TABLE OF CONTENTS

White House Council on Women and Girls
Recent Accomplishments of the Corporation for National and Community Service
March 2014

Providing Girls and Young Women an Opportunity for a Better Future Through Education, Counseling, Training and Advocacy: Through its Social Innovation Fund (SIF), CNCS provides funding for the PACE Center for Girls which operates in non-residential centers in 17 Florida counties. PACE focuses on middle and high school girls involved in, or at risk of becoming involved in, the juvenile justice system. These young women receive comprehensive case management, counseling and therapeutic treatment. They also engage in a life skills management and academic curriculum designed to help them stay out of the juvenile justice system and lead successful lives. Participants stay an average of nine to 15 months, after which they transition to another school, graduate or obtain a GED, or go on to post-secondary education or employment. Once girls leave PACE, they receive three years of follow-up services. During the time frame of the grant, PACE will serve an estimated 647 additional girls by expanding capacity in existing centers and opening two or three new service locations. Consistent with SIF's mission to invest in ideas that are effective and proven to work, CNCS we will help conduct a randomized controlled trial to test the impact of this program. This study will be one of only a few evaluations of gender-responsive programming.

Expanding Opportunities for Women and Girls in Science, Technology, Engineering, and Math (STEM). The MD Out of School Time (MOST) Network's AmeriCorps VISTA Program works to better after-school and summer opportunities, particularly for underserved students. One of MOST's primary areas of focus is STEM (Science, Technology, Engineering, and Math) programming). MOST seeks to address the gender disparity in STEM jobs by working through its AmeriCorps VISTA members to support innovative programs that expose girls to robotics and teach them to code their own apps. This work is exemplified via programs such as Robodoves and Technovation Maryland. AmeriCorps VISTA members have worked to secure funding for the Robodoves; Maryland's only all girls robotic team providing successful competitive opportunities for high school girls. Technovation Maryland was launched by an AmeriCorps VISTA member spurring statewide participation in app-building and entrepreneurship competitions for girls.

Providing Support and Financial Empowerment to Survivors of Domestic Violence. As part of an organization providing housing and support for victims of domestic violence, AmeriCorps VISTA members developed a comprehensive eight-week financial empowerment curriculum in four different languages to meet the needs of low-income survivors of domestic violence. Participants who complete this program leave with their own bank accounts, a basic understanding of borrowing and lending, budgeting resources, and information about obtaining and managing credit. AmeriCorps VISTA members also developed similar programs in job training, education and housing, and they recruited a core group of 100 qualified volunteers that contributed over 25,000 service hours to date. Volunteers provide administrative support, mentoring, language translation, group facilitation, and overall program support for program. As of June 2013, 366 people participated in the financial empowerment program.

Helping Women Start and Grow Their Own Business. Through a program called People Helping People, AmeriCorps VISTA members are working to reduce the number of children living in poverty by teaching low-income women, primarily single mothers, how to earn an adequate income through stable employment that pays a living wage. This program teaches low-income women how they can build better futures for themselves and their children by becoming, and remaining, successfully employed. The AmeriCorps VISTA project's objectives are to replicate the Salt Lake City-based program in Utah and Weber Counties, and to increase the capacity to serve more low-income women. As a result of AmeriCorps VISTA members' efforts, the program has significantly increased the number of clients it serves. In addition, the AmeriCorps VISTA members contacted and/or reactivated over 200 community agencies to educate them about the program's resources and they recruited or re-engaged more than100 volunteers.

White House Council on Women and Girls
Recent Accomplishments of the Department of Homeland Security
March 2014

Combatting Human Trafficking Through Blue Campaign. The Blue Campaign is the unified voice for DHS' efforts to combat human trafficking. Working in collaboration with law enforcement, government, non-governmental and private organizations, Blue Campaign provides information on training and outreach, victim assistance and indicators of human trafficking. Increased awareness and training will lead to more tips to law enforcement, which will result in more victims being identified. The Blue Campaign's "Out of the Shadows" public service announcement (PSA), available in English and Spanish, educates the public on how to recognize and report human trafficking   The CNN Airport Network, which broadcasts in public waiting areas in 48 U.S. airports, began featuring "Out of the Shadows" during the 2013 Labor Day weekend. The PSA ran through December and will resume periodic showings in 2014. The Blue Campaign's Blue Lightning Initiative (BLI) provides U.S. commercial airlines and their employees a voluntary mechanism to identify potential human trafficking victims and a way to notify federal authorities. U.S. Customs and Border Protection (CBP) leads the initiative with support from U.S. Immigration and Customs Enforcement (ICE), the Human Smuggling and Trafficking Center, the Federal Air Marshal Service, the Federal Aviation Administration, various non-governmental organizations, and private industry members. Since its rollout in June 2013, five airlines have committed to using the BLI, including: Allegiant Air, Delta, JetBlue, North American Airlines, and Silver Air.

Combating Violence Against Women. DHS has taken a number of steps to combat violence against women, including the following:

DHS Council to Combat Violence Against Women: Increased collaboration between the DHS Office of Intergovernmental Affairs (IGA), other DHS Components serving the Blue Campaign and the DHS Council to Combat Violence Against Women (CCVAW) has led to improved policies and programs for women and girls. IGA is committed to supporting these efforts by targeting and amplifying information and messages to state, local, tribal, and territorial elected and appointed officials, and the national associations that represent them. In 2013, the National Association of Counties (NACo) signed a Memorandum of Understanding to promote the Blue Campaign, and to increase awareness regarding human trafficking. The partnership was announced at NACo's Justice and Public Safety Steering Committee meeting on July 20, 2013. In 2013, the DHS CCVAW identified current and past initiatives, programs, and products related to protecting vulnerable women. This information was consolidated to serve not only as an internal tracking document, but also as a valuable resource for the general public to help combat violence against women.

VAWA/U Visa/T Visa Case Resolution: The Violence Against Women Act (VAWA)/T and U visa cases have been a critical focus area for the Office of the Citizenship and Immigration Services Ombudsman (the Office of the USCIS Ombudsman), which assists individuals encountering difficulty securing immigration benefits and services. For cases involving trafficking, domestic violence, and other crimes, the Office of the USCIS Ombudsman has designated an expert point of contact to facilitate communication and resolution involving U.S. Citizenship and Immigration Services (USCIS).

USCIS Ombudsman Recommendation: In 2013, the Office of the USCIS Ombudsman published a recommendation entitled "Improving the Process for Removal of Conditions on Residence for Spouses and Children," emphasizing the need for timely, appropriate adjudication and training related to waiver petitions filed for women and children who are victims of domestic violence.

T and U Visa Training: USCIS and ICE's Homeland Security Investigations Victim Assistance Program and Law Enforcement Parole Section developed and implemented comprehensive training on Continuous Presence, T and U visas, and the range of resources available for federal, state, and local law enforcement officers engaged in protecting victims of violence.

Maximizing Usage of U and T Visas: For the fourth year in a row, USCIS reached the annual statutory caps for U and T visas, which provide relief for cooperating victims, including those who have endured severe forms of human trafficking and domestic violence.

Improving Medical Care for Women in Detention. In 2012 and 2013, ICE implemented a revised set of national detention standards, entitled the 2011 Performance-Based National Detention Standards (PBNDS 2011), which include a focus on medical care for women in custody. This guidance establishes uniform minimum requirements for the provision of health care to women, including gynecological and obstetrical care. For example, detained women are entitled to routine age-appropriate medical assessments, preventive services (including baseline mammograms, pelvic examinations, pap smears, and STD screenings), birth control, and pregnancy services.

Protecting Parental Rights. In August 2013, ICE issued a directive on "Facilitating Parental Interests in the Course of Immigration Enforcement Activities," establishing a policy and procedures to ensure immigration enforcement efforts do not impede the rights of alien parents or legal guardians with minor children physically present in the U.S. The Directive focuses on parents who are primary caretakers; parents and legal guardians with a direct interest in family court proceedings in the U.S.; and parents or legal guardians whose minor children are U.S. citizens or lawful permanent residents. The Directive complements other ICE policies related to prosecutorial discretion. The Directive also designates a specific point-of-contact within each field office for parental-interest matters; establishes processes to identify and regularly review cases involving parents, legal guardians, and primary caretakers, and to determine the appropriateness of apprehension, detention or removal; facilitates participation of detainees in family court proceedings; promotes parent-child visitation; and accommodates care and travel arrangement for the children of detainees facing removal.

Protecting Unaccompanied Alien Children. DHS has taken steps to protect unaccompanied alien children, including the following:

Unaccompanied Alien Children Working Group: The DHS Office for Civil Rights and Civil Liberties (CRCL) and Office of Policy co-chair the Unaccompanied Alien Children (UAC) working group, which coordinates Components' efforts to prepare for sudden increases in migrant children, formalize permanent and effective policies and procedures, and develop best practices. The USCIS Ombudsman has also created a pilot video to educate UACs about immigration benefits and services, encourage their cooperation while in HHS or DHS custody, revises specific law enforcement training modules, and alert teens and parents in Central America of the dangers of entering the U.S. illegally.

CBP Public Awareness Campaign: CBP launched a public awareness campaign aimed at children and families in El Salvador, Guatemala, and Honduras, particularly 12- to 17-year-olds. The goal of the campaign was to dissuade potential undocumented migrants from illegally crossing the border because children, especially young girls, who migrate to the U.S. without the protection of their parents or legal guardians often face serious danger as they attempt to enter the U.S. illegally via Mexico. The campaign utilized multiple media formats to promote awareness of the potential dangers, including human trafficking, that children face while attempting to enter the U.S. illegally. The campaign was active in Central America from January to July 2013, and continues today with assistance from federal and nongovernmental organization (NGO) partners. The campaign was coordinated across DHS Components, and with interagency partners, NGO representatives, and Central American Embassy representatives to ensure that the message resonated with the target audience. Feedback from a survey conducted at the conclusion of the campaign found it to be highly credible, reaching over 73 percent of young people and their parents.

USCIS Ombudsman Recommendation: On September 20, 2012, the Office of the USCIS Ombudsman published a recommendation titled "Ensuring a Fair and Effective Asylum Process for Unaccompanied Children" to address problems involving jurisdiction determinations, interviews, and methods and approaches in the adjudication of asylum applications for unaccompanied immigrant children.

Preventing Sexual Assault and Abuse. DHS has taken numerous steps to prevent assault and abuse, including:

Improvements to the Sexual Assault Prevention and Response Program: The U.S. Coast Guard (USCG) published a Sexual Assault Prevention and Response (SAPR) Strategic Plan, which establishes goals in the following areas: climate, prevention, response, and accountability. A Military Campaign Office and Senior Level Sexual Assault Prevention Council were established to oversee implementation of the SAPR Strategic Plan. The Judge Advocate General Office of Special Victims' Counsel provides legal assistance to victims of alleged sexual assaults and other offenses. The Special Victims Counsel will care for USCG personnel and ensure victims understand their rights.

ICE's Reinforced Safeguards Against Sexual Abuse: In May 2012, ICE issued a Directive on Sexual Abuse and Assault Prevention and Intervention, which establishes a zero-tolerance policy with respect to individuals in ICE custody. This policy delineates the duties of agency employees to timely report, coordinate responses and investigations, and monitor effectively all incidents of sexual abuse or assault according to agency procedures. The Directive also requires all ICE employees who may have contact with individuals in ICE custody to receive training on sexual abuse and assault prevention and intervention. In addition, the Directive establishes a robust and multi-layered system for agency-wide review and monitoring of all sexual abuse incidents and data to promote effective oversight and evaluation of agency sexual abuse prevention and intervention issues and efforts.

DHS regulations to prevent, detect, and respond to sexual abuse and assault in DHS confinement facilities. On February 28, DHS finalized regulations implementing the Prison Rape Elimination Act of 2003 (PREA) to prevent, detect, and respond to sexual abuse and assault in DHS confinement facilities. The rule was first proposed in 2013 and was finalized after extensive public comment. The DHS rule will require extensive planning and training for officers and others who work in DHS detention facilities, as well as standards for audits and compliance reviews. The rule covers immigration detention facilities overseen by U.S. Immigration and Customs Enforcement (ICE) as well as short-term holding facilities, which are used by both ICE and U.S. Customs and Border Protection (CBP). While the rule builds on substantial DHS safeguards against sexual assault already in place, DHS will continue to develop policies, procedures, and practices that advance PREA's goal of preventing sexual abuse in confinement facilities.

Promoting Science, Technology, Engineering and Mathematics (STEM) for Women. DHS has undertaken a number of efforts to promote women in STEM, including:

In March 2013, DHS celebrated Women's History Month with a series of events related to this year's theme, "Women Inspiring Innovation through Imagination: Celebrating Women in Science, Technology, Engineering and Mathematics." Programs highlighting the impact of women in science included speakers, panels and other programming.

Supporting STEM Programs in Frederick County: The Battelle National Biodefense Institute (BNBI) – DHS National Biodefense Analysis and Countermeasures Centers management and operations contractor - has provided volunteers and funding to Maryland's Frederick County Public School (FCPS) STEM programs since 2012. BNBI donations have supported the FCPS Women in Science and Engineering (WISE) Program/Club that is designed to challenge high school women who show academic interest in STEM to learn more about STEM careers and college/university STEM departments. Currently there are about 30 women in the club with representation from all 10 county high schools.

Cybersecurity Career Workshop: On November 13, DHS Cyberskills Management Support Initiative Executive Director Renee Forney joined other cybersecurity women professionals at the annual Cool Careers in Cybersecurity for Girls Workshop at the University of Maryland, College Park. The annual event provided 300 middle school girls from the national capital region an opportunity to participate in interactive crime-solving sessions, and also network with professionals from technical companies and federal agencies.

Secret Service Recruitment Webpage: In April 2013, United States Secret Service Recruitment Division with the Office of Government & Public Affairs and Forensic Services Division created a recruitment webpage geared toward women interested in careers with the Secret Service. The page offers specific opportunities for women to serve as Special Agents, Uniformed Division Officers, and Administrative, Professional and Technical Assistants.

Secret Service Hosts College Students: In June, 2013, the Secret Service Recruitment Division hosted female college/university students on tours at the James J. Rowley Training Center, and the U.S. Secret Service Headquarters Building. Approximately 28 women from the University of Maryland, University of Baltimore, Trinity Washington University, Stevenson University, and American University attended full-day tours during which they heard perspectives and about work experiences of female Special Service personnel.

Women Veterans at DHS: In Fiscal Year 2013, slightly more than 20 percent of veteran new hires at DHS were women. In comparison, according to statistics provided by the Department of Veterans Affairs, women represent just over 10 percent of all veterans.

Training Women in Law Enforcement. Since 2012, the Federal Law Enforcement Training Centers (FLETC) has delivered the "Women in Law Enforcement Leadership Training Program" to more 404 participants from 46 countries. The training was delivered at the International Law Enforcement Academies in Bangkok, Thailand; Gaborone, Botswana; San Salvador, El Salvador; Budapest, Hungary; and the Regional Police Training Centers in Lima, Peru.

In September 2012, FLETC delivered Violence Against Women Training at the National Native American Law Enforcement Association annual conference, including three blocks of training on Human Trafficking Indicators, Violence against Women Updates related to Tribal Lands, and Investigating Domestic Violence on Tribal Lands.

Providing Training on Human Trafficking. Since April 2012, USCIS has provided training and educational materials to more than 2,000 community-based organizations, nonprofits, and faith-based groups that represent and provide victim services to women and children. USCIS has also conducted numerous in-person and web-based trainings and presentations on combating human trafficking and on immigration relief options for victims across the U.S. In addition, the USCIS Refugee, Asylum, and International Operations Directorate (RAIO) has developed a training module on trafficking that is used to train all new officers at RAIO. RAIO's Asylum Division conducted additional training for new asylum officers at the Asylum Division Officer Training Course, which is required for all newly hired asylum officers. The training covers the Trafficking Victims Protection Reauthorization Act, making UAC determinations, detecting indicators of trafficking, and what asylum officers should do if they suspect that an asylum applicant has been or is being trafficked. Each asylum office has designated a human trafficking point of contact who has connected with their local ICE Special Agent in Charge trafficking points of contact and local ICE Victim Assistance Coordinators to establish referral and information-sharing mechanisms on human trafficking-related cases.

White House Council on Women and Girls
Recent Accomplishments of the Department of Commerce
March 2014

Measuring the Economic Participation and Living Situations of Women and Girls. The Department of Commerce's Economics and Statistics Administration (ESA) releases a broad range of data measuring the economic participation and living situations of women and girls, including:

Measuring the Pay Gap: The U.S. Census Bureau's regular report on Income, Poverty and Health Insurance that showed the female-to-male earnings ratio of women working full-time, year-round remained at 77 percent in 2012.

Providing Statistics on Women's Work Histories and Their Participation in STEM Occupations: In 2013, the U.S. Census Bureau released several studies on work and earnings differentials between women and men that show the premium from educational attainment and work experience, as well as the effects of earnings by tenure. Though women's representation in STEM occupations increased since the 1970s, women remain underrepresented in most STEM occupations.

Child Care Arrangements of Working Mothers: In 2013, the U.S. Census Bureau released a report showing that in 2011, 10.9 million preschoolers lived with employed mothers, up from 8.2 million in 1985. Day care centers or nursery schools were frequented by 29 percent of young children.

Measuring the Impact of Home Production on the U.S. Economy: In May 2012, the Bureau of Economic Analysis released new statistics that adjust the measures of U.S. Gross Domestic Product (GDP) for the value of "Home Production"—that is, for the value of cooking, housekeeping, childcare, gardening, etc. The new figures show that Home Production would add approximately $3.8 trillion—or 26 percent—to GDP in 2010.

Conducting the Survey of Business Owners: In September 2013, the U.S. Census Bureau began data collection operations for the 2012 Survey of Business Owners (SBO). The SBO provides the only comprehensive, regularly collected source of information on the composition of U.S. businesses by gender, ethnicity, race, and veteran status.

Helping Women-Owned Businesses Export. In FY13, trade specialists from the Department of Commerce's International Trade Administration (ITA) participated in 33 events in 14 cities designed to provide information to women-owned business about making the most of global business opportunities. Additionally, ITA's Office of the National Export Initiative and Trade Promotion Coordinating Committee partnered with national and local business networks across the country to educate more American companies – particularly small and medium-sized enterprises (SMEs) – on the business case for exporting and federal resources to help. In fall 2012, ITA worked with a network of thousands of women-owned businesses to enhance their export education curriculum and host a webinar on starting to export and increasing export markets.

Providing STEM Opportunities for Women and Girls. The Department of Commerce, through the National Institute of Standards and Technology (NIST), the National Oceanic and Atmospheric Administration (NOAA), and the United States Patent and Trademark Office (USPTO), is working to encourage more women and girls to participate in Science, Technology, Engineering, and Mathematics (STEM) programming and careers. For example:

In 2013, the USPTO reached more than 3000 girls through targeted programming focused on intellectual property and Science, Technology, Engineering, Art, Design and Mathematics (STEAM). These programs included workshops on 3D printing, invention concepts, engineering design, product packaging, and patent and trademark protection.

During the past two summers, 126 undergraduate women (35% of the program's total enrollment) gained valuable laboratory skills by participating in the NIST Summer Undergraduate Research Fellowship (SURF) program that provides hands-on experience to students in laboratories at NIST. In that same period, NIST provided opportunities for more than 100 women science teachers to learn cutting edge measurement science as participants in the NIST Summer Institute for Middle School Science Teachers and through other educational outreach activities.

Since April 2012, the highly selective NIST/National Research Council Postdoctoral Research Associateships Program has brought women to the NIST campus for research opportunities, and women represented 27% of successful applications in NRC competitions held since April 2012 (a 6 % increase from one decade earlier).

Over the course of 2012 and 2013, NOAA hosted a number of opportunities for young women and girls to attend science workshops, camps, classes, and seminars to highlight work in the STEM fields and NOAA's mission and goals. In addition, NOAA partnered with many colleges, universities, high schools and elementary schools to promote educational opportunities for students in the environmental sciences.

White House Council on Women and Girls
Recent Accomplishments of the Department of Defense
March 2014

Opening Ground Combat Positions to Women. In January 2013, the Department of Defense (DoD) announced rescission of the 1994 Direct Ground Combat Definition and Assignment Rule prohibiting assignment of women to direct ground combat units below the brigade level, and directed the opening of all remaining closed units and positions consistent with the Joint Chiefs' Guiding Principles by January 1, 2016. Since 2012, DoD has notified Congress of its intent to open approximately 57,000 positions that were previously closed to women.

Preventing and Responding to Sexual Assault. Beginning with Secretary of Defense Chuck Hagel and Chairman of the Joint Chiefs General Martin Dempsey, DoD's leaders are committed to eliminating from the Armed Forces the crime of sexual assault, which affects both men and women. DoD has implemented a number of programs designed to prevent sexual assault in the military, and, if crimes do occur, to provide victims with the care and support they need to seek justice and heal. These include a range of initiatives designed to improve victim confidence, reform the military justice system, provide legal support to victims, enhance access to victim advocacy, and increase training and awareness for the entire force.

Promoting Women's Participation in Conflict Prevention and Resolution, and Preventing Gender-Based Violence Abroad. Pursuant to Executive Order 13595 and the U.S. National Action Plan on Women, Peace, and Security (WPS), the Department of Defense has worked to institutionalize its support for women abroad as active participants in security sector decision-making. For example, Combatant Commands including U.S. Africa Command, U.S. Pacific Command, U.S. Northern Command, and U.S. Southern Command have integrated WPS concepts into their day-to-day plans and activities, including their bilateral engagements with partner militaries and at U.S.-sponsored events at regional centers for security studies. Since August 2012, the Department has also undertaken steps to support conflict-related gender-based violence prevention and response efforts pursuant to Executive Order 13623 on Preventing and Responding to Violence Against Women and Girls Globally. These efforts include working with key foreign partners to bolster critical sexual violence prevention initiatives through NATO, the United Nations, and the Group of Eight (G8).

Advancing Women in Senior Roles Across the Department. Women in DoD continue to break barriers as senior uniformed military and civilian leaders. On December 5, 2013, President Obama appointed the Honorable Christine H. Fox as Acting Deputy Secretary of Defense, the Department's second-highest civilian official. Ms. Fox is the first woman ever to hold the position and the highest-ranking female official in Department of Defense history. Also in December 2013, the Senate confirmed the Honorable Deborah Lee James as the 23rd Secretary of the Air Force, making Ms. James only the second woman to hold the Air Force's senior-most civilian position. Finally, also in December 2013, President Obama nominated, and the Senate confirmed, U.S. Navy Vice Admiral Michelle Howard to receive a fourth star and assume the position of Vice Chief of Naval Operations. Once in her new role as Vice Chief, Admiral Howard will become the first female four-star flag officer in U.S. Navy history, and the first woman to serve as the second-ranking military officer of a uniformed service within the Department of Defense.

Increasing Employment and Educational Opportunities for Military Spouses. To assist military spouses (approximately 95% of whom are women) in reaching their educational and career goals, in fiscal year 2013 DoD supported more than 28,000 junior spouses with financial assistance through the Military Spouse Career Advancement Accounts Scholarship Program (MyCAA). To connect these and other military spouses with employers, since June 2011 DoD has partnered with Joining Forces and numerous companies through the Military Spouse Employment Partnership (MSEP). Since MSEP's inception in 2011, employers have hired more than 58,900 military spouses, far exceeding First Lady Michelle Obama's announced goal of 50,000 hired military spouses by 2015.

White House Council on Women and Girls
Recent Accomplishments of the Department of Energy
March 2014

Empowering Women in Clean Energy to Lead. The Department of Energy's Office of Policy and International Affairs continues to grow and strengthen the U.S. Clean Energy Education and Empowerment (C3E) program to advance women in clean energy. The United States is one of nine governments supporting the C3E initiative, a network of national-level actions to increase women's participation in clean energy careers worldwide. The United States is working to close the gender gap with a three-part program including an annual C3E Symposium to build a community of professional women advancing clean energy; annual C3E Awards for mid-career leadership and achievement; and the ongoing engagement of the C3E Ambassadors, a group of distinguished senior professionals who serve as spokespersons and champions. At the 4th Clean Energy Ministerial meeting in New Delhi, the C3E initiative launched C3Enet.org, an online network to connect women around the world.

Advancing Female Role Models in STEM to Promote The STEM Workforce. The Department of Energy's Office of Economic Impact and Diversity created the Women @ Energy series in March 2013, posting over 150 profiles of women in the Energy Department workforce who share their passion for STEM, their work at the Department, tips for engaging women and minorities in STEM, and their personal stories. The profiles have been featured in classrooms around the country, gaining more than 20,000 page views since the launch, and profiles are continuing to be added to the site. Additionally, in January 2014 the Department of Energy launched a #WomeninSTEM video series to highlight women in clean energy careers.

Creating a National Dialogue and Action Plan on Addressing Underrepresented Participants in the Energy Sector. The Department of Energy's Office of Economic Impact and Diversity and Secretary Moniz launched the Minorities in Energy (MIE) Initiative in 2013. The initiative aims to empower, equip, and prepare traditionally underserved businesses, communities, schools, and individuals- including women, girls, and minorities - to take advantage of the technical, procurement, engagement, workforce, and energy literacy resources of the Department of Energy and the energy sector overall. DOE hosted three well-attended events with bi-partisan participation at the Department, the White House and on Capitol Hill. The MIE Initiative has 30 Ambassadors who will begin a series of roundtables and public speaking events in 2014

Promote Women's Entrepreneurship in the Energy Sector. In November 2013, the Department of Energy's Office of Energy Efficiency and Renewable Energy's Small Business Innovation Research Program launched an outreach and education effort to increase the number of women and minority business applicants.

Convening Women on Climate Change, Finance, and Community Engagement. The Department of Energy partnered with the White House in May 2013 to host the White House Leadership Summit on Women in Climate Change and Energy, convening 150 leaders to discuss engaging diverse audiences in climate change and energy, and bringing more women into careers that tackle these fields. Breakout sessions discussed education, workplace, and community engagement on climate change adaptation, resilience, and mitigation and synergies amongst the participants to collaborate on these issues.

White House Council on Women and Girls
Recent Accomplishments of the Department of Education
March 2014

Combating Gender-Based Violence on College and K-12 Campuses: The Department of Education (ED) sent a key policy letter from Education Secretary Arne Duncan to guide Chief State School Officers in their efforts to create safer communities for young women by raising public awareness of gender based violence, educating communities about how violence affects women and youths, and encouraging new efforts to prevent and respond to violence. In FY 2013, the U.S. Department of Education's Office for Civil Rights (OCR), which enforces Title IX of Education Amendments of 1972 (Title IX), resolved **45** complaints on sexual assault/violence. OCR has also prioritized proactive investigations of sexual violence during this Administration, emphasizing OCR-initiated sexual violence investigations at a rate ten times their percentage of all complaints OCR receives. [ACS1]

Partnered With NASA to Expand STEM Opportunities. In partnership with the National Aeronautics and Space Administration (NASA), ED launched a pilot program to provide online STEM challenges to students and families via the 21st Century Community Learning Center Program (21CCLC). The 21CCLC program provides grants to states to support **academic enrichment opportunities** during non-school and extended learning time, **particularly for students who attend schools in under-resourced communities**. The pilot worked with three 21CCLC states (Colorado, Michigan and Virginia) to implement a blended training and support strategy to integrate STEM challenges and content into existing programming. By making these resources available via the 21CCLC programming structure, the pilot can reach more students who are traditionally underrepresented in STEM, including female students, minorities and students with disabilities.

Improving College Access and Readiness for Women. ED has prioritized college access and readiness through the President's 2020 goal for the U.S. to be first in the world in college graduates. To ensure that women have equal opportunities in higher education, The President has doubled our investment in federal Pell Grants benefiting the 5.1 million women who have received Pell grants since the President took office. Through the President's 5-Year Strategic Plan on STEM Education and through ongoing efforts at ED and federal research centers, the Administration has continued to support additional pathways and mechanisms of support for female scientists and engineers.

Supporting Pregnant and Parenting Students. In June 2013, the Office for Civil Rights issued a Dear Colleague Letter and Pamphlet on "Supporting the Academic Success of Pregnant and Parenting Students Under Title IX of the Education Amendments of 1972" (June 25, 2013). The letter and pamphlet, which were sent to school districts, colleges and universities across the country, contain information on effective strategies to support students who become pregnant or father children, and guidance on educational institutions' legal obligations under Title IX to support them.

Ensuring Equal Access to Athletic Opportunities. In FY 2013, the U.S. Department of Education's Office for Civil Rights (OCR) resolved **47** complaints regarding Title IX athletics. OCR's resolutions ensure that girls and boys have the same quality facilities and equal opportunities to participate in athletic programs.

Combatting Human Trafficking of School-Aged Youth. ED's Office of Safe and Healthy Students (OSHS) has undertaking a number of initiatives to raise awareness about – and ultimately prevent – domestic human trafficking among school-aged youth. ED hosted a Webinar on the commercial sexual exploitation of children in schools that reached nearly 1,000 participants nationwide. ED partnered with the Administration for Children and Families (HHS), the National Center for Homeless Education, and Grossmont Union High School District in CA. ED drafted a MOU with the Department of Homeland Security to work together on training and outreach initiatives to combat human trafficking. OSHS has also worked to educate school systems and their staffs about trafficking to increase awareness and reporting.

White House Council on Women and Girls
Recent Accomplishments of the Department of Interior
March 2014

Working to Decrease Violence Against Women in Native Communities. Rates of violence against women in Indian Country are alarmingly high. The Violence Against Women Reauthorization Act of 2012 allows tribes to exercise sovereign power to investigate, prosecute, convict and sentence both Indians and non-Indians who assault Indian spouses or dating partners or violate a protection order in Indian country. The legislation eliminates the legal loopholes that prevented the arrest and prosecution of non-Indian men who commit domestic violence against Indian women on Federal Indian lands. As a part of these efforts, in 2013, the Department of the Interior (DOI), the Bureau of Indian Affairs (BIA), and the Department of Justice trained more than 300 tribal court personnel in trial court advocacy skills with specific emphasis on issues affecting the safety of Native Women. Furthermore, thanks to legal, institutional and educational initiatives and BIA's priority goal of reducing crime on targeted reservations, rates of violent crime -- of which women are disproportionately the victims have dropped significantly on reservations across the country.

Involving Young Women in Environmental Stewardship. Agencies across the Department of Interior have supported and implemented youth programming to provide opportunities for students to learn about America's natural resources. The National Park Service's (NPS) Air Resources Division partnered with Girl Scouts of the USA to provide lessons on science and environmental stewardship, and to date, 1,958 Girl Scouts have logged more than 13,000 volunteer hours in parks across the country. In addition, the Office of Surface Mining, Reclamation and Enforcement/Volunteers in Service to America (OSM/VISTA) teams have placed 238 young professional women (out of about 382 total positions, or 62%) in capacity-building roles with numerous nonprofits in rural mining communities impoverished by environmental degradation.

Documenting and Preserving Women's History in Our National Historic Landmarks. Beginning in May 2012, a new Secretarial initiative focusing on women's history was introduced, with the goal of documenting, preserving, and protecting important sites associated with women's history. Doing so enriches and enhances our understanding of our shared history as a nation. New designations and documentations range from Camp Nelson, Kentucky (designated 2012) to which thousands of African American women fled with their families during the Civil War to the Harriet Beecher Stowe House, Connecticut (designated 2012), the site where Stowe played a crucial role in the women's rights movement.

Supporting Women's Participation in Science, Technology, Engineering and Mathematics (STEM) Fields. Agencies across the Department of Interior have implemented various programs to encourage women to pursue careers in STEM fields. Support for these STEM education programs particularly benefits girls since so many are otherwise "counseled out" of STEM fields. Examples of programs include the following:

The longest running STEM internship program in the nation, which is co-sponsored by the U.S. Geological Survey (USGS) and the National Association of Geoscience Teachers. More than 2,200 students have participated in this program, with an impressive number of participants moving on to distinguished careers with the USGS, academia, or industry. While the majority of these interns go on to graduate school, over one-third who have participated in the program became permanent hires of USGS.

A partnership between USGS and the Alaska Native Science and Engineering Program to increase the number of indigenous American students pursuing STEM degrees.

A partnership between USGS and the University of Texas, Jackson School of Geosciences, to support the GeoFORCE program, a unique, longitudinal program targeting minority, first generation high school graduates, that has an impressive record of college admission and matriculation into STEM fields.

The National Ocean Sciences Bowl program, a national high school academic competition on the ocean that is co-sponsored by the Bureau of Ocean Energy Management (BOEM). About 1,000 girls (half of the total number of students involved) participate annually in the competition.

Encouraging Women to Lead Healthier Lives. During 2013, the NPS partnered with GirlTrek, a nonprofit organization with more than 15,000 participants and 300 volunteers that encourages African American women and girls to lead healthy lifestyles. GirlTrek offers a Summer Trek series for women at parks like Yosemite, Great Smoky Mountains, and Shenandoah. In addition, DOI supports efforts in Indian schools to improve young women's health. Examples include 1) BeLieving In Native Girls (BLING) at Riverside Indian School in Anadarko, Oklahoma, which is an HIV- prevention initiative funded by the Office on Women's Health. During the past seven years, more than 500 adolescent girls aged 12 to 18 years of age have participated in this nine-month program, and 2) A partnership between the Bureau of Indian Education and the Indian Health Service to educate girls in Wingate High School in Ft. Wingate, New Mexico about health, domestic violence, alcohol and drug abuse, HIV/AIDS prevention, and safety.

Opening Child Care Center in Interior Headquarter. In November 2012, Interior opened a brand new child care center in the Main Interior Building. Built in partnership with GSA (General Services Administration), the center is the first federal day care to be LEED platinum certified.

Announced Goals to Bridge the Growing Disconnect between Young People and the Great Outdoors. In October 2013, Secretary of the Interior Sally Jewell announced an ambitious initiative to inspire millions of young people to play, learn, serve and work outdoors. As part of the initiative, young women will benefit from the 100,000 work and training opportunities on public lands that Secretary Jewell aims to create through public-private partnerships.

White House Council on Women and Girls
Recent Accomplishments of the Department of Justice
March 2014

Reauthorizing the Violence Against Women Act. On March 7th, 2013, President Obama signed the Violence Against Women Reauthorization Act (VAWA) of 2013 which maintains programs that reduce domestic and sexual violence and expands and improves the federal government's response to violence against women. VAWA 2013 includes provisions that support the sovereignty of American Indian and Alaska Native tribes and hold perpetrators accountable – a necessary step to reducing violence against Native women. The reauthorization of VAWA also ensures that lesbian, gay, bisexual and transgender survivors have access to the services they need and deserve; enables victims in publicly subsidized housing to stay safe by transferring to a different unit or location; and adds protections for college students, who experience some of the highest rates of rape in the nation. Altogether, VAWA authorizes nearly $500 million each year, administered by the Office on Violence Against Women, to reduce domestic violence and sexual assault.

Protecting Women's Civil Rights. The Civil Rights Division at the Department of Justice (DOJ) continued to aggressively enforce the federal laws protecting the civil rights of women, ensuring equal employment opportunities for women in the workplace, holding accountable perpetrators of sexual assault, and securing justice on behalf of victims of sex trafficking. In 2013 alone, the Division obtained more than $875,000 dollars in monetary relief and damages for victims of workplace sex discrimination. The Division also reached settlement agreements with the University of Montana and the Missoula, Montana Police Department to ensure that women will be protected from sexual assault and harassment. And in cases such as United States v. Fields and United States v. Alaboudi, the Division convicted traffickers who preyed on vulnerable young women, using addictive drugs to manipulate and compel their victims to engage in commercial sex.

Improving Sexual Assault Forensic Examinations. On April 12, 2013, Attorney General Eric Holder released the updated "National Protocol for Sexual Assault Medical Forensic Examinations, Adult/Adolescent" (SAFE Protocol, 2nd edition). The revised SAFE Protocol uses the latest information and best practices to improve the quality of services victims receive. When followed, the Protocol also improves the quality of forensic evidence collected, enhances law enforcement's ability to collect information and file charges, and increases the likelihood of successful prosecution. DOJ also released a companion protocol to improve responses to sexual assault in prisons and other correctional environments ("Recommendations for Administrators of

Prisons, Jails, and Community Confinement Facilities for Adapting the U.S. Department of Justice's A National Protocol for Sexual Assault Medical Forensic Examinations, Adults/Adolescents"). Both protocols address populations with special needs, such as victims with limited English proficiency; victims with disabilities; American Indian and Alaska Native victims; victims in the Military; and lesbian, gay, bisexual, and transgender victims.

Protecting Women in the Federal Workforce. On November 20th, 2013, DOJ released a new policy to address domestic violence, sexual assault, and stalking in the workplace. DOJ was the first major federal agency to submit a final workplace policy in response to the April 2012 Presidential memorandum requiring each federal agency to develop and implement a policy to prevent domestic violence and address the effects of domestic violence on its workforce. DOJ's policy helps victims keep their jobs through clearly described flexible leave options, enabling them to attend a protection order hearing or visit a mental health professional. The policy also includes provisions that hold offenders accountable with disciplinary actions and security procedures, and it addresses complex situations, such as when a perpetrator and victim who work in the same building – or even the same office.

Pioneering Approaches to Save Women's Lives. On March 13, 2013, Vice President Biden and Attorney General Holder announced the first-ever Domestic Violence Homicide Prevention Demonstration Initiative grant awards to 12 cities and counties totaling $2.3 million. The Office on Violence Against Women is partnering with the National Institute of Justice to rigorously evaluate the implementation and outcomes of this initiative, which is based on successful homicide reduction models in Massachusetts and Maryland. These models use a short list of screening questions to identify victims who may be in fatally abusive relationships. Once at-risk victims or offenders are identified, law enforcement, prosecution, courts, and service providers can take action to protect victims and their families. This team of responders can search for open warrants, make arrests, connect victims with services, and use pretrial conditions to keep offenders in custody.

Releasing National Academies' Report: Confronting Commercial Sexual Exploitation and Sex Trafficking of Minors in the United States. In 2013, the National Academies' Institute of Medicine and the National Research Council released an Office of Juvenile Justice and Delinquency Prevention (OJJDP)-sponsored report on sexual exploitation and sex trafficking of U.S. citizens and lawful permanent residents under 18. The $1.5 million, OJJDP-funded study found that "despite the serious and long-term consequences for victims as well as their families, communities and society, efforts to prevent, identify, and respond to these crimes are largely under supported, inefficient, uncoordinated, and unevaluated." The Committee found that minors who are victims of these crimes may be arrested, detained, and given permanent records as offenders under current law. The report provided recommendations on how to address this issue.

Improving the Juvenile Justice System's Response to Girls. The Office of Juvenile Justice and Delinquency Prevention (OJJDP) supported multiple projects to better meet the needs of girls in the juvenile justice system. Projects include an effort to improve services for system-involved girls and develop gender-responsive, trauma-informed policies and practices and a study to better understand the impact of juvenile justice system involvement on adolescent maturation, trajectories of delinquency, and young adult adjustment among females. OJJDP will also evaluate the Young Women Leaders Program, a one-on-one and group-based mentoring program to prevent delinquency and related outcomes in at-risk girls.

Using Telemedicine to Reach Underserved Victims of Sexual Assault. Sexual assault victims have unique medical, emotional, and forensic needs that require a trauma-informed approach; however, many communities do not have access to sexual assault nurse examiners (SANE) and related expertise. Telemedicine — technologies that provide care from a distance — can expanding access to these resources while significantly reducing costs. The Office for Victims of Crime (OVC) and the National Institute of Justice, along with the Massachusetts Department of Public Health SANE Program, the U.S. Navy, and the Indian Health Service, are working to develop the first telemedicine center to provide remote expert consultation to clinicians caring for adult and adolescent sexual assault patients. The center will set up pilot projects at two military medical facilities in California and Florida to perform telemedicine consultation during sexual assault forensic exams. Future sites will include rural jurisdictions and correctional facilities.

White House Council on Women and Girls
Recent Accomplishments of the Corporation for Department of Labor
March 2014

Establishing Minimum Wage and Overtime Protections for Direct Care Workers. In September 2013, the Department of Labor announced a final rule that extends Fair Labor Standards Act (FLSA) minimum wage and overtime protections to most direct care workers. Direct care workers are the certified nursing assistants, home health aides, personal care aides, caregivers and companions who provide private in-home care services to elderly people and people with illnesses, injuries or disabilities. Of the nearly two million workers who are affected by this final rule, approximately 90 percent are women.

Expanding Family and Medical Leave Policies. To mark the 20th anniversary of the Family and Medical Leave Act (FMLA) in February 2013, the Department of Labor announced a final rule that includes two important expansions of FMLA protections. The first expansion provides families of eligible veterans with the same job-protected FMLA caregiver leave available to families of military service members and enables families of Reserve and National Guard members to take up to 12 work weeks of leave for activities that arise when a family member is deployed. The second expansion modifies existing FMLA eligibility rules to allow airline personnel and flight crews access to FMLA protections.

Enforcing Equal Pay and Protecting Women in the Workforce. Over the past several years, the Department of Labor has devoted significant enforcement resources to investigating and remedying cases of pay discrimination, discrimination against women, and labor violations in industries in which women are likely to work. Since 2010, DOL has closed more than 90 cases of pay discrimination and recovered approximately $3.3 million in back pay for more than 1400 Federal contractors. In addition, the Department has recovered nearly $335 million in back pay for more than 475,000 workers in low-wage industries, including industries in which the workforce is predominately comprised of women.

Establishing a Veterans Employment and Training Service (VETS) Program for Women Veterans. In November 2013, the Department of Labor established a Women Veteran Program aimed at serving the nation's 2.3 million women veterans. The program educates women veterans about the availability of the American Job Centers and other DOL resources for veterans in the workforce. It also helps businesses better understand the strengths and challenges women veterans bring to the workplace and informs them of best practices in recruiting and retaining women veterans .

Creating a Workplace Flexibility Toolkit. The Department of Labor recently unveiled a Workplace Flexibility Toolkit which provides valuable information to employees, employers, policymakers and researchers about workplace flexibility strategies. The toolkit, which is available through the Department's website, includes case studies, fact and tip sheets, issue briefs, reports, articles, websites, link to other toolkits and answers to frequently-asked questions.

White House Council on Women and Girls
Recent Accomplishments of the Department of Transportation
March 2014

Providing STEM Training and Educational Opportunities. The Department of Transportation continues to partner with WTS, International to implement Transportation YOU, a career exploration program for girls ages 13 to 18. Since the launch of Transportation YOU in 2012, more than 600 girls have participated in the program, which is coordinated by 30 WTS chapters across the country. In addition, USDOT and WTS jointly host a leadership summit in Washington, DC focused on helping seniors in high school focus on post-secondary opportunities. Approximately 80% of the 35 girls who have participated in the Leadership Summit have reported that the program has had an impact on their career aspirations and their focus of study as they enter college.

Fighting to End Human Trafficking. The Department of Transportation has led the development of Transportation Leaders Against Human Trafficking (TLAHT), which now includes more than 90 transportation organizations working to put an end to human trafficking in the U.S. and around the world. In addition, in 2013, all DOT employees participated in a training to learn the signs of potential trafficking. DOT has also worked closely with the Department of Homeland Security to launch the Blue Lightning Campaign with Amtrak, Delta, JetBlue and others. DOT is in the process of working with TLAHT to develop tools and materials that can be used by various modes of transportation to continue raising awareness about this issue.

Making the Business Case for Women in Transportation Leadership at Home and Abroad. As a result of DOT's leadership, the Asian Pacific Economic Corporation's Transportation Ministerial Meeting featured a women's forum for the first time last year, including more than 175 participants representing all 21 APEC member countries. During the forum, panelists discussed the positive effect that the increased participation of women has on growth, sustainability, and the economic competitiveness of the transportation sector throughout the APEC region. Based on Forum outcomes and recommendations, APEC Transportation Ministers directed the continuation of the effort, and individual organizations and economies are currently adopting measures to expand opportunities for women in transportation. Sample activities include: 1) Vietnam's organization of a National Congress on Women in Transportation and a resulting collaborative national action strategy aimed at increasing the number of women in transportation leadership, and 2) a group of local transportation leaders in Memphis organizing a scholarship for women pursuing transportation-related professions at the

University of Memphis. Next steps will center on developing a framework to exchange best practices, enhance data collection and build capacity. Building on this momentum, DOT hosted a White House Forum with senior US transportation industry executives to begin to define the 'business case for women in transportation'. During this session, participants discussed best practices, tools and strategies needed to advance women in transportation careers. Then-Secretary LaHood also held two separate roundtables with senior level executives and board members to specifically identify strategies for advancing women into CEO and Board level positions. DOT is continuing to partner with WTS to continue this effort.

Recruiting Women into Skilled Transportation and Infrastructure Careers. The Department of Transportation continues to work closely with stakeholder organizations, including SkillUp Washington, Legal Momentum, Wider Opportunities for Women, and Oregon Tradeswomen to identify best practice strategies to recruit women into transportation and infrastructure jobs where they are seriously underrepresented, including jobs in trucking, construction, maritime, rail, and buses. DOT also continues to support on-the-job training for women in transportation through the Federal Highway Administration's On-The-Job Training Initiative.

Helping Families Travel More Safely. Safety is the Department of Transportation's (DOT's) top priority, and DOT strives to provide women and their families with the tools to help them make informed decisions when traveling. Over the last two years, DOT has created the SaferBus and SaferCar apps, free tools that help consumers research a bus company's safety history before buying a ticket or learn about a car's safety features while shopping for new vehicles. The SaferCar app also features information on the nearest site where families can find help installing a car seat. Over 23,922 people have download SaferCar app since its launch.

White House Council on Women and Girls
Recent Accomplishments of the U.S. Environmental Protection Agency
March 2014

Keeping Women Informed About Safe Fish Consumption Choices. In 2004, EPA and the FDA jointly advised women who may become pregnant, pregnant women, nursing mothers, and young children to avoid some types of fish and to eat fish that is low in mercury. EPA is continuing to work with communities that rely heavily on subsistence fishing, in which unhealthy levels of mercury in infants persist. To address this problem, EPA provided more than $5 million dollars during 2012 and 2013 through the Great Lakes Restoration Initiative to fund projects that will reduce mercury exposure in women of childbearing age in the Great Lakes region.

Closing Racial and Ethnic Gaps in Childhood Asthma Rates. Roughly 7 million children (including 3 million girls) are affected by asthma, especially minority children and children with family incomes below poverty level. Asthma rates of African American children are around 16%, while 16.5% of Puerto Rican children suffer from the chronic respiratory disease – more than double the rate of Caucasian children in the U.S. In addition, of the 16 million adults with asthma in the U.S., more than 10 million are women – with asthma deaths nearly twice as prevalent among women, especially among women over 35. In May 2012, the President's Task Force on Environmental Health Risks and Safety Risks to Children released a Coordinated Federal Action Plan to Reduce Racial and Ethnic Asthma Disparities to improve asthma care and health outcomes. In the two years since the launch of the Plan, EPA has supported training for about 16,000 health care providers to equip them to deliver comprehensive asthma care, and partnered with the Ad Council to launch a new social media-based series of public service announcements (in English and Spanish) to help parents, caregivers and youth learn about simple steps they can take in their own homes to eliminate indoor environmental asthma triggers and prevent asthma attacks (www.noattacks.org).

Increasing Women's Opportunities for STEM Training in Indian Country. Since 2011, EPA's Tribal ecoAmbassadors Program has created new STEM opportunities for more than 100 tribal college students. The program, which partners Tribal College and University (TCU) professors and students with EPA scientists to solve pressing environmental issues, has provided more than 60 tribal college women with the opportunity to develop professional monitoring and analysis skills critical for an environmental career.

Creating Healthier Indoor Environments in Schools and Childcare Facilities. Of the 3.7 million teachers in elementary and secondary public schools in the U.S., 76% are women, as are nearly 95% of the 2.3 million day care providers – many of whom are of childbearing age. Studies have found that indoor air quality problems in our nation's schools are widespread. EPA has been working since the mid-1990s to provide guidance, outreach, and technical support to states, schools and other childcare settings to promote the adoption of indoor air quality management plans to correct and prevent such problems. Data from the 2012 Centers for Disease Control School Health Policies and Practices Study indicates that nearly half of the school districts in the U.S. are implementing indoor air quality management programs to protect the health of students and staff – the majority of which are based on EPA's *Indoor Air Quality Tools for Schools* guidance. Since 2012, EPA has been working with national, state and local non-profit organizations to reach the other half of the nation's schools where students and teachers are still learning and working in sub-optimal environments.

Educating Female Farm-workers of Childbearing Age About Pesticide Exposure. Farm worker populations in the U.S. are comprised mainly of Spanish-speaking individuals (81%) and approximately 21% of these individuals are women, the vast majority of whom are of childbearing age. Since April 2012, EPA has partnered with the Association of Farmworker Opportunity Programs, a worker advocacy organization, to develop a training curriculum that educates women farm workers of childbearing age about the specific risks associated with pesticide exposure when pregnant, and about steps they can take to avoid exposure. To date, 40 stations in seven states have aired public service announcements related to this project. In 2014, the project will be expanded to include a pesticide safety training curriculum in partnership with the Association of Opportunities Programs for female farm workers who are pregnant or who may become pregnant.

Providing Safer Cook Stoves to Improve Women's Health. More than half the world's population, and approximately 75% of households in developing countries, cook their food and heat their homes by burning coal and other solid fuels over open fires or rudimentary stoves, leading to indoor air pollution levels that are 20 to 100 times greater than the World Health Organization's (WHO) air quality guidelines. WHO estimates that roughly 4 million people, primarily women and children, die prematurely each year from exposure to indoor smoke. Today, EPA funds and works closely with the Global Alliance for Clean Cookstoves, a United Nations Foundation initiative that was launched by the EPA Administrator, the Secretary of State, and other federal agency and global leaders in 2011 to expand the work of the EPA-led Partnership for Clean Indoor Air. To advance the Alliance goal of having 100 million homes using demonstrably improved cookstoves by 2020, Alliance members provided 8.2 million improved cookstoves in 2012, enabling more than 40 million people, primarily women and children, to live healthier lives.

Supporting Women-Owned Small Businesses (WOSB). On March 5, 2013, the EPA Office of Small Business Programs (OSBP) hosted its annual Women-Owned Small Business Counseling Session. This counseling session was designed to educate WOSBs on how to do business with EPA, provide WOSB's with access to EPA contracting officers and program office representatives, and provide WOSBs an opportunity to network. Later in 2013, OSBP supported

WOSB outreach conferences held by the U.S. Women's Chamber of Commerce, providing training and information on contracting opportunities at EPA. As a result of these efforts to support WOSBs in FY 2013, EPA met the federal WOSB 5% goal, with an achievement of 5.74% (as reported from the Federal Procurement Data System-Next Generation, as of 9/30/13). This translated into $89.4 million in contracts awarded to WOSBs.

Protecting Women and Families from Exposure to Pests and Pesticides in Schools. Through partnerships and grant programs, EPA is working to create safer, healthier learning environments for children and families through use of school Integrated Pest Management (School IPM). Advancing the adoption of School IPM's commonsense approach to pest management helps create healthier indoor settings with reduced risk from exposure to pests and pesticides (which is particularly important for the health of women and children, who are especially vulnerable to chemical and environmental risks). EPA has committed more than $1.1 million in support of school IPM implementation including assistance agreements focusing on Ohio, Indiana, Wisconsin, Florida, Georgia, Alabama, Louisiana (City of New Orleans), Colorado, Utah, Oregon and Washington State. Since May 2012, more than 2 million K-12 public school students across the nation have benefited from expanded implementation of school IPM, and EPA is currently seeking to award an additional $.06 million for school IPM projects that will affect an additional 2.5 million K-12 public school students.

Focusing Research and Policy Decisions with Comprehensive Data on the Effect of Contaminants on Children. In 2013, EPA released the third edition of "America's Children and the Environment," its latest and most comprehensive compilation of information on children's health and the environment. The report shows trends for contaminants in air, water, food, and soil that may affect children; concentrations of contaminants in the bodies of children and women of child-bearing age; and childhood illnesses and health conditions. The national indicators presented in this report can help identify areas that warrant additional attention through research, data collection, and policy decisions. More on "America's Children and the Environment, Third Edition": http://www.epa.gov/ace/

White House Council on Women and Girls
Recent Accomplishments of the Corporation for Federal Trade Commission
March 2014

Announcing Key Consumer Protection Settlements that Stop False, Deceptive or Unfair Marketing Practices for Products Bought by Hundreds of Thousands of Women. Consumers can count on the FTC to ensure that claims made by marketers meet the legal standards for truthfulness, accuracy and substantiation. Among the highlights:
Apple, Inc., will provide $32.5 million in refunds to settle an FTC complaint that the company billed consumers for millions of dollars of charges incurred by children in kids' mobile apps without their parents' consent. Under the settlement, Apple also will change its billing practices to make sure it gets express, informed consent from people before charging them for items sold in mobile apps. (Jan. 15, 2014)

In Operation Failed Resolution, the FTC stopped national marketers that used deceptive advertising claims to peddle fad weight loss products from food additives and skin creams to dietary supplements. The marketers of Sensa, who exhorted consumers to "sprinkle, eat and lose weight," will pay $26.5 million to settle the charges; the FTC will make these funds available for refunds to consumers who bought the product. Other companies charged with making unfounded claims include L'Occitane, which said its skin cream would slim user's bodies; HCG Direct, which marketed an unproven human growth hormone that has been touted by hucksters for 50 years as a weight loss treatment; and LeanSpa, which allegedly promoted acai betty and "colon cleanse" weight loss supplements through fake news sites. (January 7, 2014)

The FTC charged Down to Earth Designs, Inc., with making deceptive claims about its Diapers product's biodegradability and compostability, among other attributes. The company settled with the FTC, agreeing not to make green claims unless they are true and not misleading, can be adequately substantiated, and meet specific requirements in the FTC's Green Guides. (Jan. 17, 2014)

The FTC went to court to shut down a telemarketing scheme that allegedly targeted Hispanic consumers with false promises that they could make money by reselling high-end merchandise from manufacturers like Gucci and Ralph Lauren, and then charged them at least $400 up-front for shoddy, off brand products. The FTC also alleged that the telemarketers, who did business under various names including Oro Marketing, threatened and intimidated consumers who refused to pay with arrest and phony lawsuits. (Jan. 2, 2014)

White House Council on Women and Girls
Recent Accomplishments of the General Services Administration
March 2014

Enhancing Childcare Through Development Centers. GSA currently provides space in federal buildings for 104 child care centers nationwide. GSA's childcare centers participate in the Let's Move Child Care (LMCC) program and altogether, these centers provide close to 8,000 children with nutritious meals and daily opportunities for physical activity. These centers provide thousands of women and working parents re-entering the workforce with the peace of mind of knowing that their children are receiving healthy, safe, high-quality care.

Helping Women Grow Their Businesses. GSA met and exceeded the 5% statutory goal for prime contracting dollars designated to Women-Owned Small Businesses (WOSB's) for two consecutive years and awarded more than $500 million to these companies. As a result of these awards, more WOSB's were able to build capital, grow their business, create jobs and remain competitive in the federal marketplace.

Increasing Telework Opportunities to Ensure Work/Life Balance. GSA is a Telework pioneer and currently has a workforce participation rate to 80%. This achievement reflects the Agency's commitment to enhancing work-life balance in order to create a more engaged, resilient and productive workforce.

Expanding Opportunities for Women in Leadership Positions. GSA has made great strides in appointing women to core leadership positions within the Agency. Women currently hold just under 50% of the SES (Senior Executive Service) and Grade 15 leadership positions in all areas of concentration including business lines and staff offices. Many of these positions include non-traditional roles such as technology and finance.

Helping Federal Agencies Create a Balanced Workplace. GSA has partnered with agencies across the federal government to help them develop strategies to create more balanced workplaces. These strategies enable agencies to reduce costs, operate efficiently, assess workplace performance more effectively, and create better work spaces for employees. As a result, employees are better able to manage their work schedules and family obligations.

White House Council on Women and Girls
Recent Accomplishments of the Department of Health and Human Services
March 2014

Providing Access to Expanded Coverage for Women under the Affordable Care Act. Under the Affordable Care Act, the Department of Health and Human Services developed guidelines requiring non-grandfathered health insurance plans to cover certain preventive services specifically for women – including contraception, screening and counseling for interpersonal violence, breastfeeding support and counseling, and well woman visits– without charging a co-pay, co-insurance, or a deductible beginning in plan years starting on or after August 1, 2012. Based on data from the Census Bureau and information from the Kaiser Family Foundation's Employer Health Benefits Survey, an estimated 26.9 million women now have expanded access to these kinds of recommended preventive services without cost-sharing. All private health insurance plans offered through the Health Insurance Marketplace also offer a set of essential health benefits, including maternity and newborn care. And today, 18.6 million women who are uninsured are now able to find insurance that fits their needs through the Marketplace.

http://aspe.hhs.gov/health/reports/2013/PreventiveServices/ib_prevention.cfm
http://www.flickr.com/photos/hhsgov/8735402755/in/set-72157633968047018

Enhancing National Intimate Partner and Sexual Violence Survey Findings on Victimization by Including Sexual Orientation. In 2013, CDC released the first set of national prevalence data on intimate partner violence (IPV), sexual violence (SV), and stalking victimization by sexual orientation. The study found that lesbians and gay men reported IPV and SV over their lifetimes at levels equal to or higher than those of heterosexuals. The survey also found that bisexual women (61.1 percent) report a higher prevalence of rape, physical violence, and/or stalking by an intimate partner compared to both lesbian (43.8 percent) and heterosexual women (35 percent). Of the bisexual women who experienced IPV, approximately 90 percent reported having only male perpetrators, while two-thirds of lesbians reported having only female perpetrators of IPV.
http://www.cdc.gov/media/releases/2013/p0125_NISVS.html

Providing Culturally Competent, Accessible, and Integrated Health Care. The Health Resources and Services Administration's Health Center Program provides funding to more than

1200 organizations that operate more than 9000 service delivery sites. In 2012, health centers provided culturally competent, comprehensive quality primary care to 21.1 million medically underserved individuals; of this number, more than 12 million (59%) were female and more than 7.7 million (62%) were between the ages of 20 and 64. Some 500,000 women received prenatal care at health centers across the U.S, 70 percent of whom began this care in the first trimester, an increase of five percent from 2008. Female health center patients are less likely to have low birth weight babies (7.14% of live births) compared to the U.S. national average of 7.99%.

Reporting a Significant Decline in Teen Births. In 2012, HHS found that birth rate for teenagers aged 15-19 dropped to 29.4 per 1,000 -- the lowest rate ever reported for the U.S. Rates were down for age groups 15-17 and 18-19, and for nearly all race and Hispanic origin groups. This rate has fallen by over one-half since 1991, when the long-term decline in births to teens began. Record lows were reached for both younger (15-17) and older (18-19) teens. Since 1991, the rate for teens aged 15-17 has fallen 63%, and the rate for teens aged 18-19 has fallen 45%. Among racial and ethnicity groups, rates for teenagers aged 15-19 declined for all groups from 2011 to 2012.

http://www.cdc.gov/nchs/data/nvsr/nvsr62/nvsr62_09.pdf

Reducing Disparities among Minority and Underserved Women. The Offices of Minority Health and the National Coordinator for Health Information Technology developed the Reducing Cancer Among Women of Color Challenge, an app challenge to create a tool for mobile devices that provides women with high-quality health information about prevention, screening, and treatment of breast and gynecologic cancers. The challenge was a first-of-its-kind effort to address health disparities among minorities. In May 2013, $100,000 in prizes was awarded to the top four winners. In August of 2013, the app challenge and first place winner were featured in O, The Oprah Magazine, which has a U.S. circulation rate of approximately 1.95 million.

Supporting Home Visiting Services for Parents with Young Children. The Health Resources and Services Administration's Maternal, Infant, and Early Childhood Home Visiting Program (MIECHV) supports voluntary, evidence-based home visiting services to parents with young children from pregnancy to age five. Providers in the community work with parents to build the skills to help take better care of their children and families. They also address issues such as intimate partner violence, mental and behavioral health issues such as peripartum depression, and economic self-sufficiency. The program is now serving more than 80,000 mothers and children in 656 counties across all 50 states, DC, and five territories.

Increasing Access to Comprehensive, Credible Online Health Information. The Office on Women's Health (OWH)'s *womenshealth.gov* and *girlshealth.gov* websites feature credible information on a vast array of health topics, reaching more than 2 million users each month. In 2013, OWH began transforming the sites into responsive design to make them easy to view and navigate, whether accessed from a desktop, tablet, or smartphone. OWH also provides personalized responses to women and girls' health questions through the OWH Helpline, which responded to more than 13,000 inquiries in 2013. Furthermore, OWH uses social media to disseminate information and engage with women and girls; cumulatively, OWH has more than

1,080,000 followers through Twitter, 27,700 followers through Facebook, and 380 followers through YouTube.

Promoting Breastfeeding Initiation and Maintenance. In 2013, HHS launched *It's Only Natural*, a campaign to promote breastfeeding among African-American mothers. This campaign provides tools, information, and personal stories to help women overcome challenges, find support, and fit breastfeeding into their lives. The campaign has been widely disseminated through print and online media, with nearly 13,000 views of the videos since the April launch. OWH also offers the only national breastfeeding helpline, through which trained breastfeeding peer counselors answer questions and offer support by phone. The helpline provided support to 3,776 mothers and their families over 2013.

Improving Screenings for Intimate Partner Violence. The HHS Coordinating Committee on Women's Health hosted the *2013 Intimate Partner Violence Screening and Counseling: Research Symposium*, which convened federal employees, researchers, practitioners, and advocates to examine the challenges and barriers to screening and intervention for intimate partner violence (IPV). The information from the symposium will inform research on gaps in IPV screening and counseling in primary health settings and shape research priorities. In addition, the OWH-funded initiative *Project Connect* continued to create partners between the violence against women and public health fields to improve clinical practice and policy in public health programs. The second phase, *Project Connect 2.0*, launched in 2013 with 11 additional sites covering adolescent health, sexual and reproductive health, and Native American communities. To further support communities in this effort, OWH created a fact sheet for health care providers on screening and counseling for interpersonal and domestic violence, which was viewed online over 6,000 times in 2013.

Continuing Pregnancy Assistance Fund with 17 New Grantees. In 2013, the Office of Adolescent Health awarded the second cohort of Pregnancy Assistance Fund (PAF) grants. A total of $22,019,937 was awarded to 14 States and three Tribes for a four-year period. Established by the Affordable Care Act (Public Law 111-148), the PAF funds States and Tribes to provide expectant and parenting teens, women, fathers, and their families with supportive services. The program identified the inclusion of services to fathers and expectant male partners as a priority for this cohort, along with linkages to existing services including education and enrollment for health care coverage, health literacy, and trauma-informed care.

Providing Assistance to Domestic Violence Survivors and Their Children. The Family Violence Prevention & Services Act (FVPSA) Program is working to improve how domestic violence programs, community based organizations, and federal agencies offer trauma-informed support to our nation's most vulnerable families. This work has led to increased awareness, access to resources, the implementation of evidence-based programming, and stronger coordination in local communities. The National Center on Domestic Violence, Trauma & Mental Health (NCDVTMH) facilitates collaboration among domestic violence advocates, mental health and substance abuse professionals, disability rights organizations, and a variety of community-based service providers, as well as government agencies at the state and national levels. Over the past year, the NCDVTMH has conducted 21 trainings that reached a total of over 1350 attendees and sponsored a webinar series that reached 800 participants.

Improving the Standard of Care and Forensic Examination for Sexual Assault Victims. The Indian Health Service (IHS) Forensic Healthcare Program trains health workers to conduct medical forensic care for American Indian and Alaska Native victims of sexual assault, intimate partner violence, child maltreatment, and elder abuse. In 2013, IHS launched its tribal forensic healthcare website (www.ihs.gov/forensichealthcare), which offers training on domestic and sexual violence to medical providers through webinars and a web-based learning system. The virtual training project provided free continuing education credits to more than 300 health care providers. Additionally, 46 IHS and Tribal hospitals and clinics received equipment to aid in the clinical documentation and evidentiary collection during sexual assault medical forensic examinations.

Working at the Intersection of HIV/AIDS and Violence Against Women. The Department of Health and Human Services plays a primary role in the White House's Interagency Federal Working Group on the Intersection of HIV/AIDS, Violence Against Women and Girls, and Gender-Related Health Disparities. HHS representatives (from Office on Women's Health/Office of the Secretary and Office of Women's Health/CDC) led the development of the research workshop, hosted webinars to engage with community stakeholders, developed collaborative implementation strategies based on the recommendations, and planned the release of the report developed by the Working Group. HHS is currently leading efforts to track progress in accomplishing the goals as directed by the Presidential Memorandum and will soon release a skills enhancement guide that addresses the link between violence against women and Increased risk of HIV.

White House Council on Women and Girls
Recent Accomplishments of the Department of Housing and Urban Development
March 2014

Implementing the 2013 Reauthorization of the Violence Against Women Act (VAWA) to Better Assist Women in HUD-Assisted Housing. The 2013 reauthorization of VAWA contains expanded housing protections for victims of domestic violence. HUD has begun to implement these changes by issuing a notice in August 2013 alerting the public of how the changes will impact tenants and housing providers in HUD-assisted housing and shelters.

Graduating Families Primarily Headed by Women from Welfare Assistance. In 2012, 3,400 families graduated from the Family Self-Sufficiency program, meaning that they were free of welfare assistance and employed. 33% of graduates no longer needed rental assistance and 15% of graduates went on to purchase a home. Over 90% of FSS participants are women in female-headed households.

Fighting Lending Discrimination Against Women. In 2013, HUD continued to aggressively investigate and resolve cases where women experienced lending discrimination because they were pregnant or on parental leave. HUD settled a total of 28 cases in 2013, obtaining almost $300,000 for 43 complainants. As a result of these investigations, some of the country's largest lenders have changed their policies and practices on maternity leave lending decision making, and Fannie Mae and Freddie Mac have updated their mortgage guidelines to remove unnecessary lending barriers to women on parental leave.

Providing Housing and Services for Victims of Domestic Violence. Through the FY 2012 Continuum of Care Competition, HUD awarded $46.7 million dollars to continue 349 projects that predominately serve victims of domestic violence. The average award amount was $134,028. Additionally, 28 new projects were awarded that predominately serve victims of domestic violence for a total of $2.6 million dollars.

Working to Re-integrate Formerly Incarcerated Women. HUD is a member of the Federal Interagency Reentry Council Women and Reentry Workgroup which has created a strategic approach to focusing on the needs of incarcerated and returning women. HUD in collaboration with the Office of National Drug Crime and Policy (ONDCP) has drafted their first series of reports profiling housing and reentry successful efforts. The purpose of the *What's Working: Housing & Reentry* series is to showcase promising approaches Public Housing Authorities (PHAs) and their local collaborators have developed to provide housing and support to individuals who are returning to the community following incarceration. Five of the six programs profiled serve women, and the MOMS program in Oakland, California serves women only. Two of the six programs also provide services and supports for the children of program participants.

Programs to Support Children of Incarcerated Parents. Children with an incarcerated parent can experience significant negative consequences including financial instability, changes in family structure, shame, and social stigma. However, research also shows that supporting healthy and positive relationships between these vulnerable children and their families can help mitigate negative outcomes. An interagency group that includes the Departments of Justice, Health and Human Services, Housing and Urban Development, Education, and Agriculture as well as the Social Security Administration, has partnered with stakeholders both inside and outside of government to identify opportunities to support these children and their caregivers. See this factsheet for further information about these efforts: http://csgjusticecenter.org/wp-content/uploads/2013/06/COIP-Fact-Sheet-2013-06-19.pdf.

http://findyouthinfo.gov/youth-topics/children-of-incarcerated-parents

Telling the Story of Women Veterans without Secure Housing. In September 2013, HUD participated in a BlogTalk Radio broadcast entitled, "Speak Up: Combating Barriers to Fair Housing for Women Veterans; Stories of Home: Homelessness, Housing Discrimination and Housing Support." This online live discussion and call-in broadcast featured issues about housing, homelessness, and reintegration for women veterans. The broadcast engaged previously homeless women veterans, expert housing practitioners, advocates, service providers, and HUD staff, examining the intersection of unfair housing discrimination practices and their impact on the problem of homelessness in the veteran community. HUD outreach resulted in more than 2,000 persons tuning into the broadcast.

HUD's Policy, Development and Research Undertakes Studies Focusing on Families. HUD is undertaking new research that focuses on families with children that have spent at least 7 days in a homeless shelter. The demonstration tests 3 different forms of rental assistance that HUD might use to help them.96% of households have either a single female adult (66 %) or at least two adults, at least one of whom is female (30%). First, HUD is undertaking a pilot study measuring discrimination against families with children in rental housing. The pilot study will inform the design of a national study of discrimination in rental housing against families with children. HUD is also undertaking research to ascertain the impact of various service and housing interventions in ending homelessness for families. HUD's Family Options Study includes over 2,200 homeless families from 12 communities randomly assigned to one of four interventions to be tested. Both the head of households and a cohort of over 2,800 children will be surveyed to assess outcomes of different service and housing interventions.

White House Council on Women and Girls
Recent Accomplishments of Millennium Challenge Corporation
March 2014

Continuing to Operationalize Groundbreaking *Gender Guidelines and Operational Procedures* (Gender Milestones). The *Gender Guidelines and Operational Procedures* codify gender integration at every step of compact development and implementation from foundational studies leading to project designs; in implementation contracts; and during monitoring and evaluation. For the first time, compact development that began in 2013 started integrating Gender Milestones into every step of the process.

Developing a New Gender Assessment. MCC developed the *Initial Social and Gender Assessment* (ISGA), now conducted at the beginning of the compact development process to assess the country-specific social context and the links among social inequality, poverty reduction and economic growth. The ISGA examines how cultural beliefs and preferences, social norms and practices, formal and informal institutions, and legal and policy frameworks affect constraints to growth and the ability of particular social groups, including women, to participate in and benefit from growth-focused investments. The ISGA was conducted in the compact development process for Liberia, Niger, Tanzania, and Sierra Leone and in the Threshold Program development process for Guatemala and Nepal.

Including Accomplishments for Women in the Mongolia Compact. The Mongolia Compact which closed in 2013, included the following accomplishments:

A property rights project included a dedicated public outreach, education and awareness-raising campaign on the importance of women registering land in their own names: Women now make up over 40 percent of those registering land, with a higher figure in urban areas. Going forward, government data on land registrations will be sex-disaggregated through the electronic property registration system, an important step toward sustaining efforts to monitor women's land ownership.

Women, particularly those in female-headed households, were strongly represented among the beneficiaries of the subsidy for energy-efficient stoves. Energy-efficient products resulted in time and cost savings for women as the stoves consume less fuel.

A substantial number of Mongolian women benefited from MCC-funded national campaigns, check-ups and screenings for diabetes, hypertension, breast and cervical cancer, and received HPV vaccinations. Women made up 60 percent of those who were screened and over 80 percent of those who received medical staff training targeting health professionals. Given the male-specific challenges in non-communicable disease prevention and the differential risk taking behavior among men, the health project also supported trainings in male-dominant workplaces like construction and mining. It also facilitated access to screenings for non-communicable diseases for more than 10,000 persons with disabilities in Ulaanbaatar.

A vocational education project promoted non-traditional career paths with higher-earning potential, such as in mining and construction, among female students. Careers counselors at educational institutions received training on gender and on trafficking in persons, enabling them to consider these issues in their work. The road project supported opportunities for women's employment in construction sites. A nationwide women's leadership campaign promoted and celebrated women's economic accomplishments and leadership through compact activities.

Including Accomplishments for women in the Lesotho Compact. The Lesotho Contract, which closed in 2013, included the following accomplishments:

The compact's Gender and Economic Rights Program met over 100 percent of its targeted training and outreach activities: 6192 of the aimed-for 6,000 people received training on gender and economic rights, including the police; traditional leaders; judicial officers; local government officials and members of youth, faith-based and community-based organizations. Public outreach activities reached 11,409 of the 10,800 people the compact targeted.

Under a joint grant and advocacy program with PEPFAR, 16 groups of women have been awarded grants valued at $300,000 for income-generating projects.

Several groundbreaking legal reforms took place to give effect to the provisions of the Legal Capacity of Married Persons Act 9/2006, an earlier compact accomplishment that abolished the minority status of married women. These include: Companies Amendment Act 7 of 2008 to allow women to be directors of companies without the consent of their husbands; Land Amendment Act, incorporated into the Land Act 11 of 2008, which provides for joint titling of immovable property; and Lesotho Bank Amendment Act 13 of 2008, which enables women to apply for credit without the consent of their husbands.

The Gender and Economic Rights Program spearheaded a joint initiative with the United Nations Population Fund and the Christian Council of Lesotho on the joint Statement of Commitment by Religious Leaders on Gender Equality in Lesotho, a critical tool to help attain gender equality in the country. The Gender and Economic Rights Program facilitated the establishment of the Federation of Lesotho Women Entrepreneurs, an independent women's economic empowerment body that works to integrate Basotho women and women entrepreneurs into economic activity nationally, regionally and globally, and also influences relevant policy and legislation and their implementation.

Including Accomplishments for Women in the Cabo Verde Compact. The Cabo Verde Compact, which was implemented in 2013, included the following accomplishment:

Design studies were completed for the water and sanitation project in the second Cabo Verde Compact and significant institutional reforms are underway for achieving social and gender equity objectives in the water and sanitation sector, addressing service delivery, planning infrastructure projects, and implementing tariff reforms.

The compact drove the creation of a new national water and sanitation agency that will have a dedicated social and gender unit as well as social and gender mainstreaming across all departments. These efforts will address access, affordability and social inclusion throughout the sector. This mainstreaming will include policymaking, planning, budgeting, and staffing across the three major national agencies responsible for the sector, and capacity building for engaging civil society organizations in these processes.

White House Council on Women and Girls
Recent Accomplishments of the National Aeronautics and Space Administration
March 2014

Expanding Women@NASA. The Women@NASA website (http://women.nasa.gov) expanded to include a second and third year of inspirational videos sharing stories of women across all NASA centers. NASA added 66 life stories that have been shared in numerous classrooms across the US and internationally. For example, in November of 2013, NASA shared the story of Dr. Tahani Amer (http://women.nasa.gov/tahani-amer) with approximately 200 students and teachers at Prince Mohammed University in Saudi Arabia, during a virtual speaking engagement. Since April of 2012, the website has attracted thousands of visitors and garners dozens of speaker requests which are fulfilled in their entirety.

Encouraging Women in STEM through the MissionSTEM Web Site. In November 2012, NASA launched "MissionSTEM," a Web site designed to assist NASA grant recipients (universities, science museums, and science centers) across the country meet their obligations under civil rights laws, including Title IX. The website enables NASA to broaden the reach of its civil rights technical assistance to our grantees, augmenting civil rights compliance reviews. In addition to describing the baseline civil rights requirements for NASA grant recipients, MissionSTEM encourages diversity in STEM (Science, Technology, Engineering and Math) fields by sharing promising practices of leading universities. The Web site features university presidents and provosts describing the importance of diversity in STEM fields, including gender diversity, and how to achieve it. Link: http://missionstem.nasa.gov/

Engaging Girls in STEM and Inspiring Them to Pursue STEM Careers. NASA has created a number of programs designed to get girls excited about STEM and inspire them to pursue careers in STEM fields. Highlights include:

In June of 2012, the NASA GIRLS pilot program was organized pairing up approximately 20 female mentors across the agency with 20 young girls in grades 5-8 across the United States. The 20 students were selected randomly from over 1600 entries, which were received after minimal promotion using social media. Each one-on-one pair met, virtually for five weeks for one hour per week to work on an assignment in science, technology, engineering, and math. In June of 2013, the mentoring program was expanded to include NASA BOYS, and the total participation grew to more 150 pairs of students and mentors from more 1300 entries received.

The NASA GIRLS/BOYS programs (http://women.nasa.gov/nasagirls) are performed on a volunteer basis with a budget of zero dollars.

During the period of April 2012 to present, NASA created and supported more than 22 events and programs focused on Robotics and STEM, impacting more 40,000 students in grades 4 through 12, including all-girls robotics teams (a number of which are in underserved areas) in various competitions. For girls participating in the high school programs, 100% go to college, and 91% pursue STEM degrees. Students participating in the robotics programs have contributed more 4,000 volunteer hours in community service.

The NASA Science, Engineering, Mathematics and Aerospace Academy (SEMAA) is a national education project designed to increase the participation and retention of historically underserved and underrepresented K-12 youth, including girls, in STEM. During FY 2012, the NASA SEMAA project served 6,278 girls (direct participants) in NASA-related, hands on, inquiry based STEM curriculum. During FY 2013, the project served an additional 8,348 girls, for a total of 14,446 girls served between Apr 2012 and Oct 2013.

The NASAScience4Girls and Their Families initiative partners libraries with NASA science educators to engage girls and their families in STEM. Each individual partnership develops events that use field-tested, hands-on educational activities; NASA resources; and librarian training provided by the science education team. In 2013, the Science4Girls collaboration partnered 42 libraries with 28 NASA science educator teams. These libraries hosted a total of 73 events across 22 states. An example was a Google+ Hangout in Spanish that highlighted the contribution of Hispanic women at NASA and was attended by 1,225 participants from seven countries, had 3,657 views of the archived video (as of Dec 18, 2013), and was covered by more than 30 web news sources. In an event in rural Butler, MO, a NASA education ambassador even attracted an audience of over 321 in a town with population just over 4,000. One participant said, "Before it was over, the community had proudly come together. Everyone was thrilled by the opportunity to host a NASA event here where nothing of this sort had ever been done before."

The NASA Summer of Innovation (SoI) project – launched in 2010 in response to the President's Educate to Innovate campaign – provides STEM education opportunities to underserved/ underrepresented students, including targeted programs for girls. SoI partners with summer and other out-of-school time (OST) programs to build the capacity of school- and community-based organizations; strengthen summer programming, increase STEM education capabilities with NASA support; and facilitate the infusion of NASA content into summer and OST learning to address local needs. Since 2012, through SoI, NASA has partnered with a number of youth organizations targeting girls including: Girls Inc., Girl Scouts, Girls Get It!, Girlstart, Chattanooga Girls Leadership Academy, JMU Female Leaders, and all-girl camps (robotics, YMCA, B&GC, 4-H). During this period, SoI engaged more than 100,000 middle school students in rising grades four to nine and 10,000 educators in NASA STEM inquiry-based experiential content. The majority of the students served by SoI were from underserved/underrepresented populations.

White House Council on Women and Girls
Recent Accomplishments of the National Science Foundation
March 2014

Published Key Report on Women, Minorities and Persons with Disabilities in Science and Engineering. Mandated by the Science and Engineering Equal Opportunities Act (Public Law 96-516), the 2013 report data organized around six themes—enrollment, field of degree, employment status, occupation, academic employment, and persons with disabilities. This report is a major source of information for the country about women in STEM fields and is used extensively by researchers, educators, and policy makers. http://www.nsf.gov/statistics/wmpd/

Awarded Graduate Research Fellowships to a Diverse Group of Students. In 2013, NSF awarded a majority of the Graduate Research Fellowships to women; of the 2,000 recipients, 1102 of them are women (55%).

Promoted Family-Friendly Practices through the Career-Life Balance (CLB) Initiative. Instituted in 2012, NSF's CLB Initiative is an ambitious, ten-year effort to take the best family-friendly practices among individual NSF programs and implement them across NSF. In FY 2013, NSF worked to advance more women in Science and Engineering Careers by offering supplemental funding opportunities within the Graduate Research Fellowship Program (GRFP), the Increasing the Participation and Advancement of Women in Academic Science and Engineering Careers (ADVANCE) Program, the Faculty Early Career Development Program (CAREER), and to postdoctoral researchers funded through NSF grants. Supplemental funding for the GRFP and CAREER programs offers additional gender-neutral funding for medical and family leave, salary support for additional research assistants. In the case of ADVANCE, supplement funds are awarded to institutions to, for example, facilitate dual-career hires on campuses attracting diverse talent to their professoriate. http://www.nsf.gov/career-life-balance/

Hosted the Third Gender Summit. Established in 2011, the Gender Summit has become the foremost forum for engaging top-level researchers, policy makers, science and innovation leaders, and other and stakeholders in STEM to address gender issues in research and innovation. The aim of the third Gender Summit, which was focused on North America, was to connect all relevant stakeholders in a Call to Action to improve diversity in the Science, Technology, Engineering and Mathematics (STEM) workforce and leadership, and to promote greater inclusion of biological sex and gender considerations or the "gender dimension" in research content and process. On-demand video recordings of the event are available at: http://www.tvworldwide.com/events/nsf/131113/

White House Council on Women and Girls
Recent Accomplishments of the Office of Personnel Management
March 2014

Mobilizing the Federal Workforce for STEM-Related Outreach and Educational Activities. OPM partnered with Federal agencies and the Office of Science and Technology Policy to promote creative ways to engage Federal STEM professionals in outreach and educational activities to build talent pipelines for future recruitment into Federal service. OPM trained and mobilized 1,067 Federal STEM professionals to engage students from all segments of society, including minorities and women, in STEM careers through curriculum development, educational activities, job shadowing, and mentoring. These efforts reached 4,472 students, many of them minorities and/or females, who participated in hands-on activities, lectures, competitions, science festivals and other innovative programming that brings STEM from the classroom into real-life applications.

Establishing the Pathways Programs for Interns and Recent Graduates. The Pathways Program was made effective on July 10, 2012. It consists of three programs designed to recruit qualified interns, fellows and employees to the federal government:

Internship Program: For current students (high school, college, vocational/technical schools and other qualifying educational institutions).

Recent Graduates Program: For recent graduates who have completed, within the previous two years (additional time applies for veterans if needed due to their military obligations), a qualifying associates, bachelors, masters, professionals, doctorate, vocational, or technical degree or certificate from a qualifying educational institution.

Presidential Management Fellows (PMF) Program and PMF-STEM: The PMF Program is the Federal Government's flagship leadership development program where advanced degree selectees complete a prestigious 2-year fellowship. For individuals who have completed a qualifying advanced degree (e.g., masters or doctorates) within the past two years (or by August 31 of the current academic year). In addition to the traditional PMF program, which draws applicants from a variety of disciplines, OPM is piloting a STEM track to attract graduate students in STEM disciplines into the public sector through the PMF Program. In 2012, President Obama asked agencies to close the skills gap for mission critical positions in STEM disciplines, and this effort is part of OPM's response to that call. As a result of increased targeted outreach efforts, in FY 2013, the percentage of female PMF-STEM semi-finalists was 54 percent.

Helping Agencies Recruit and Retain a Diverse Workforce. OPM Provided leadership and support to agencies by issuing an extensive update on its *Human Resources Flexibilities and Authorities in the Federal Government* handbook in August 2013. This handbook gives agencies guidance on how to strategically use their limited resources to recruit and retain a diverse and high-performing workforce,

Supporting Federal Telework Programs. OPM has continued its commitment to supporting robust Federal telework programs. In addition to providing training and guidance to Federal telework coordinators and Telework Managing Officers, the Work-Life and Performance Culture staff has conducted annual Telework Data Calls, the most recent of which resulted in the release of the *2013 Status of Telework in the Federal Government Report to Congress* in December 2013. As shown in this report, Federal telework participation continues to increase. More women than men reported teleworking in 2011 (24 percent versus 18 percent) and 2012 (27 percent versus 21 percent). More men reported facing barriers to telework in 2011 (70 percent versus 65 percent) and 2012 (66 percent versus 61 percent). Notably, however, there is an encouraging trend toward more teleworkers among both groups, with fewer women or men reporting a barrier to telework in 2012 than in 2011. A copy of the report can be found at: http://www.telework.gov/Reports_and_Studies/Annual_Reports/2013teleworkreport.pdf.

Federal Women's Leadership Summit and Activities. In celebration of Equal Pay Month, the Equal Pay Task Force, in collaboration with the U.S. Office of Personnel Management (OPM), the U.S. Equal Employment Opportunity Commission, the U.S. Department of Labor, and the U.S. Department of Justice, hosted the Federal Women's Leadership Summit (the Summit) and follow-up activities. The Summit sought to empower women to confidently pursue the knowledge, skills, and relationships they will need to develop and mature as successful Federal leaders. It also provided a forum for women who have achieved leadership and executive stature in Federal service to give back to those who aspire to their positions through mentoring, role-modeling, networking, and advocacy roles.

In June 2013, the Summit focused on Engaging Women to Advance in their Federal Careers; Gender in Negotiation and Leadership; Women in the Senior Executive Service; and Creating a Gender Inclusive Workplace. In August 2013, a webcast, with over 2,000 Federal employee viewers nationwide, provided an overview of the Federal leadership journey by emphasizing the Executive Core Qualifications (ECQs) and steps an individual can take when preparing for the Senior Executive Service. Another webcast, this time in conjunction with an in-person session, was held in September 2013, with over 1,200 Federal employee viewers nationwide, covered topics on mentoring/ coaching/ sponsorship and career planning.

Expanding Government-wide Veteran Hiring. Under the President's Veterans Employment Initiative (Executive Order 13518), the Government is experiencing an increase in the percentage of Female veterans in the Federal workforce. The percentage of female veterans on board in the Federal work went from 16.7% in 2010 to 18.3% in 2012. Several important efforts implemented through the President's Initiative are contributing to this increase:

Feds Hire Vets Web and Social Media Outlets
- Focused information on Federal employment to the veteran community
- Targeted recruitment of veterans eligible for special noncompetitive appointments specifically designed for veterans
- Marketing of other special hiring authorities to Veteran Services Organizations (including women-focused veteran services organizations) such as the PMF Program, Schedule A for individuals with severe disabilities, and the Pathways Program for Interns and Recent Graduates.

Veteran Employment Program Offices in 24 Federal Agencies
- Veterans have an advocate for promoting Veterans' recruitment, employment, training and development, and retention within these respective agencies
- Veterans can contact an real individual for specific information on employment opportunities in those agencies

Vets to Feds (V2F) Career Development Program
- Sponsored by the Interagency Council on Veterans Employment
- Recruits our Nation's Student Veterans and Recent Graduates for careers with the Federal Government
- Designed to fill some of the Government's most important and critical positions; Contracting and IT to date.

In FY 2012, the Executive Branch of Government hired the highest percentage of veterans in over 20 years, surpassing the previous high set in FY 2011. The Government hired approximately 195,000 new employees in FY 2012 as compared to approximately 230,000 new employees in FY 2011-a reduction of over 34,000 total hires. Of those 195,000 FY 2012 hires, approximately,56,000 were veterans, equaling 28.9 percent of total hires. This was a 4.9 percentage-point increase over the FY 2009 baseline of 24.0 percent and approximately 0.6 percentage points higher than the 28.3 percent hired in FY 2011.

OPM-SPECIFIC ACCOMPLISHMENTS:

Creation of WorkLife4You. WorkLife4You is an Employee Assistance Program Concierge Service that provides information for employees, eldercare services, and kits (including a pre-natal kit, childcare safety kit, off to college kit, be-well kit, and adult care kit) with useful information and free products to help employees and their household members with every stage of life. The eldercare services include three free hours in person with a Geriatric Care Professional and unlimited telephonic access. WorkLife4you also offers free moderated discussion groups for employees dealing with eldercare issues, parents of children with special needs, parents of teens, and professional development.

Helping Agencies Support Nursing Mothers. Released in January of 2013, OPM's *Guide for Establishing a Federal Nursing Mother's Program* details the legislative requirements under the Patient Protection and Affordable Care Act that Federal agencies must meet in support of nursing mothers. This comprehensive guide also demonstrates the benefits of breastfeeding to agencies, mothers, and their nursing infants. In the guide, agencies can find guidance on how to develop a program from the ground up and specific information on how an agency can improve and sustain an existing program. In addition, several Federal agencies with outstanding nursing mother's programs are highlighted for benchmarking purposes. OPM's Work-Life and Performance Culture staff also provides ongoing guidance and support to agencies developing their lactation programs in order to help women maintain their employment and produce an environment that is inclusive of those with family responsibilities. A copy of the guide can be found at: http://www.opm.gov/policy-data-oversight/worklife/reference-materials/nursing-mother-guide.pdf.

Developed Federal Agency-Specific Policies to Address Domestic Violence, Sexual Assault, and Stalking. In accordance with the Presidential Memorandum released on April 18, 2012, OPM coordinated an inter-agency working group to develop and release the *Government-wide Guidance for Agency-Specific Domestic Violence, Sexual Assault and Stalking Policies* in February 2013. The Guidance provides information for agencies on the key components required for effective policies to combat the effects of domestic violence, sexual assault, and stalking on the Federal workforce. OPM's Work-Life and Performance Culture staff has provided continued support to agencies in developing their policies, including hosting three webinars for agency policy teams, with topics such as responding to domestic and sexual violence in the workplace; training, awareness, and partnership considerations; and disciplinary actions and legal considerations. In addition, OPM reviewed and provided structured feedback on 50 agency and component policy drafts. http://www.opm.gov/policy-data-oversight/worklife/referencematerials/guidance-for-agency-specific-dvsas-policies.pdf.

Expanding Access to Family-Related HR Guidance. The OPM Pay and Leave office assisted employees in being better able to access family-related HR guidance by establishing two new "one-stop" pages on OPM's website: a (1) leave and families page (http://www.opm.gov/policy-data-oversight/pay-leave/leave-administration/fact-sheets/leave-and-families/) to address the wide variety of leave-related benefits available to employees, including domestic partners, to help them balance their work and family obligations, and (2) a military-related leave page (http://www.opm.gov/policy-data-oversight/pay-leave/leave-administration/fact-sheets/military-related-leave-issues/) that provides, among other things, information on leave-related topics for employees with military family members.

Creating a Federal Work-Life Community of Practice. To assist Federal agencies in developing and implementing work-life programs – including workplace flexibilities, telework, dependent care programs, health and wellness programs, and Employee Assistance Programs – the Work-Life and Performance Culture staff has created a Federal Work-Life Community of Practice on www.max.gov. Created in 2012, this website is a valuable resource for Federal agency coordinators of work-life programs, and it includes resources, discussion boards, event calendars and more to ensure high-quality Federal programs and sharing of knowledge and best practices among Federal agencies. As of December 2013, the Work-Life Community of Practice had over 430 members government-wide.

White House Council on Women and Girls
Recent Accomplishments of the Peace Corps
March 2014

Enhancing Gender Equitable Teaching Practices and Schools to Combat Gender-Based Violence. More than 1000 Peace Corps (PC) Volunteers in the education sector have received training that gives them the skills to work with their in-country counterpart teachers to introduce more gender equitable practices into the classroom routine and create safe spaces for all children to learn. To date, 113 host country national staff in Africa and Asia have received training on gender equitable teaching practices and addressing gender based violence at the community level. In addition, every Peace Corps trainee at every PC post worldwide receives one hour of gender training as part of pre-service training.

Providing Agency-wide Sexual Assault Policy Training. 100% of Peace Corps staff have completed training in sexual assault awareness and victim sensitivity. Staff at Peace Corps headquarters and 66 overseas posts are equipped with the knowledge and skills to respond to sexual assault and gender-based violence.

Providing Fellowship, Mentorship and Professional Development Opportunities for Women. In 2013, the Peace Corps established Women's Empowerment at Peace Corps (WE@PC), an inclusive group that will provide fellowship, mentoring and professional development opportunities within and beyond employment at Peace Corps for all women employees. The group hopes to begin a formal relationship with the organization Federally Employed Women (FEW).

White House Council on Women and Girls
Recent Accomplishments of the Corporation for U.S. Small Business Administration
March 2014

Helping More Women Obtain Federal Contracts. In 2011, to help increase women's participation in the federal contracting space, the Small Business Administration (SBA) implemented the Woman-Owned Small Business (WOSB) Federal Contract Program, allowing contracting officers to set-aside contracts with competition that would be limited to WOSBs. In FY 2012, SBA awarded $16.2 billion of federal small business eligible contracting dollars to WOSBs. The National Defense Authorization Act of 2013 removed the caps on the contracts that were eligible for this program, and in 2013 SBA worked quickly to implement the cap removal, allowing contracting officers to set aside contracts with higher dollar amounts. To further support women in the federal contracting space, SBA, in partnership with Women Impacting Public Policy (WIPP) and American Express OPEN, created the ChallengeHER campaign in 2013. The goal of this campaign is to increase awareness of federal opportunities available to WOSBs.

Increasing Women's Access to Capital. Between January 2009 and December 2013, SBA made 57,831 loans worth $17.2 billion to women-owned businesses. In 2013 alone, SBA made $3.8 billion in capital available to women, a 31% increase since 2009. SBA has also improved its policies around underwriting loans worth $350,000 or less, which could help increase the number of loans to women-owned businesses.

Helping Women Start and Grow Their Own Businesses. SBA's national network of more than 100 Women's Business Centers offer women comprehensive training and counseling to help them start and grow their own small businesses. These centers trained and counseled more than 270,000 entrepreneurs in FY12 and 13, many of them in underserved and economically disadvantaged areas. SBA's Women's Business Centers, Small Business Development Centers, and SCORE chapters counseled and trained over 850,000 women in FY12 and 13.

Helping Women Veterans Start and Grow Businesses. In 2012, SBA launched the *Boots to Business: from Service to Startup* initiative to provide entrepreneurship training for transitioning service members. I In 2013, SBA reached more than 1,300 women veterans with this initiative and plans to reach even more in 2014. SBA also expanded its Veteran Women Igniting the Spirit of Entrepreneurship V-WISE program, which was launched in 2011 to provide women veterans with intensive entrepreneurship training. In 2012 and 2013, SBA completed six V-WISE programs in cities across the country, serving nearly 1,000 female veterans and military spouses. Each participant completed more than 30 hours of instruction, and after the training, more than half of the participants who were in the nascent or start-up phases of their businesses reported starting or continuing to grow their business within the first year. This is projected to increase to more than 70 percent within 3 years of completing the program.

Helping Encore Entrepreneurs Start and Grow their Businesses. In May 2012 SBA and AARP entered into a strategic alliance to jointly counsel, train or mentor more than 100,000 new and existing encore entrepreneurs (entrepreneurs over the age of 50). As of December 2013, this program has provided small business training to 119,268 new and existing encore entrepreneurs, more than half of whom are women.

White House Council on Women and Girls
Recent Accomplishments of the Department of State
March 2014

Investing in Gender Integration with the Full Participation Fund. In March 2013, Secretary Kerry announced the Full Participation Fund, coordinated by the Secretary's Office of Global Women's Issues, to support bureaus' and embassies' innovative efforts to integrate gender in operations, diplomacy, and development.

Expanding Interagency Efforts to Combat Trafficking in Persons. Following President Obama's call to action at the 2012 meeting of the Clinton Global Initiative in New York, agencies comprising the President's Interagency Task Force to Monitor and Combat Trafficking in Persons (PITF) have worked to deliver on an ambitious agenda to combat modern day slavery both at home and abroad, including by expanding services and legal assistance available to victims; strengthening protections in federal contracts; training federal prosecutors, law enforcement officials, and others; and establishing innovative public-private partnerships.

Preventing and Responding to Gender-based Violence:

Launching the Safe from the Start Initiative. Continuing the U.S. commitment to prevent gender-based violence (GBV) and implement the U.S. Strategy to Prevent and Respond to Gender-based Violence Globally, the State Department, in conjunction with USAID, launched the *Safe from the Start* initiative in September 2013. The initiative aims to increase the capacity of the international humanitarian response system to prevent and respond to GBV from the very onset of an emergency – not as an afterthought, but as standard practice. The initiative includes a $10 million initial investment from the Department of State's Bureau of Population, Refugee, and Migration (PRM) for organizations such as the Office of the United Nations High Commissioner for Refugees (UNHCR) to train and hire staff and develop innovative programs to protect women and girls in emergencies.

Championing International Efforts to End Gender-based Violence in Conflict. The United States drafted and negotiated UN Security Council resolution 2106 on conflict-related sexual violence, which reinforces the Security Council's efforts to prevent such violence, hold perpetrators accountable for their crimes, and provide support and justice to survivors. Furthermore, the United States demonstrated strong support for the United Kingdom's Preventing Sexual Violence Initiative (PSVI), including through the G-8 through a $10 million dollar commitment to programs that prevent, respond to, and advance justice and accountability for GBV in armed conflict and post-conflict situations; and at the United Nations General Assembly, where the U.S. signed on to the September 2013 Declaration of Commitment to End Sexual Violence in Conflict.

Promoting Gender Equality through PEPFAR Investments. Through the President's Emergency Plan for AIDS Relief (PEPFAR), the United States is working to strengthen health systems and enhance the capacity of countries to prevent and respond to gender-based violence. Over the past four years, PEPFAR has reached over 114,000 individuals with post-exposure prophylaxis (PEP) to prevent HIV for sexual violence survivors in 19 countries.

Providing Emergency Assistance to Survivors of Gender-based Violence. Launched in the fall of 2013, the Gender-Based Violence Emergency Response and Prevention Initiative is a public-private partnership between the U.S. State Department's Bureau of Democracy, Human Rights, and Labor (DRL), Vital Voices, and the Avon Foundation. Through ten regional hubs, this initiative provides emergency assistance to survivors of extreme acts of gender-based violence, including harmful traditional practices. In addition, the fund offers targeted prevention and/or protection assistance to GBV organizations. To bolster these efforts, the Avon Foundation is providing support for dynamic trainings to spur the implementation of anti-GBV laws in three target countries. The initiative also coordinates and strengthens a global network of GBV first responders.

Supporting Sexual and Reproductive Health Programs. The United States, with the support of the Congress, is the world's largest donor of sexual and reproductive health assistance, providing approximately $610 million in FY 2013, which includes over $36 million for United Nations Population Fund (UNFPA). The U.S. government's partnership with UNFPA supports sexual and reproductive health information and services, including voluntary family planning, in over 150 countries. Since 2009, the United States has provided over $200 million to UNFPA for life-saving assistance to women, children, and families, including for those in crisis settings such as Syria and the Philippines.

Combating Trafficking in Persons. The State Department is undertaking a number of efforts to fight human trafficking both at home and abroad, including:

- **Advancing the Fight Against Human Trafficking Globally.** On June 19, 2013, Secretary Kerry released the 2013 *Trafficking in Persons Report*, which ranked 188 countries and territories – including the United States – on their governments' effectiveness in combating trafficking in persons. The Report provided recommendations for how governments can improve their response to this crime and highlighted the importance of enhanced efforts to identify victims. Media coverage of the Report reached an all time high – in its 13-year history – raising public awareness of human trafficking globally.

- **Expanding Human Trafficking Training Within the State Department.** The Office to Monitor and Combat Trafficking in Persons and the Foreign Service Institute worked together to create an interactive training to ensure State Department personnel understand the signs of human trafficking and their obligations to report it. The training includes case examples, provides information on the Department's standards of conduct related to human trafficking, and outlines where to report human trafficking or related activities. The training also highlights the Department's policy prohibiting the procurement of commercial sex even in countries where it is legal.

- **Addressing Child Trafficking in Haiti.** Combining diplomacy with foreign assistance, the State Department's Office to Monitor and Combat Trafficking in Persons engaged Haitian officials at the highest levels to improve the response to trafficking and supported programs to prevent child trafficking and identify and assist child victims. Through the Office's programs, more than 1,000 child victims of trafficking have been provided with comprehensive care, including family tracing and reunification, and a grassroots model program to reduce the number of children entering domestic servitude has been created in communities that have been a source of child victims. These efforts have diminished the social acceptance of this practice and reduced the number of children living in domestic servitude.

- **Recognizing the Extraordinary Efforts of Leaders in the Anti-trafficking Movement.** The first-ever *Presidential Award for Extraordinary Efforts to Combat Trafficking in Persons* was presented to two recipients who have led efforts to combat trafficking in the United States and globally. Florrie Burke, a leading advocate for a victim-centered approach to combating human trafficking and catalyst in the anti-trafficking movement in the United States, and Carlson, a global hospitality and travel company, received Presidential medals that commemorate their accomplishments and efforts. The driving force behind Carlson's leadership on this issue was Marilyn Carlson Nelson, who personally used her voice and platform to advance the issue within the travel, tourism, and hospitality sector.

Preventing and Responding to Gender-based Violence in Specific Regions. The State Department works in countries around the world to prevent and respond to gender-based violence through a comprehensive and multi-sector approach. For example:

Africa:

- In the Democratic Republic of the Congo (DRC), a mobile court program administered in collaboration with the American Bar Association, with support from the Bureau of International Law Enforcement and Narcotics (INL), resulted in 381 trials and 305 convictions for GBV-related offenses. INL also funds Physicians for Human Rights to provide medical support to GBV survivors, including training medical and legal service providers on the use of GBV kits to gather evidence for prosecution.

- Special Envoy to the Great Lakes Region of Africa, with the support of the State Department's Office of Global Criminal Justice, engaged in robust diplomacy to ensure that a UN-brokered peace agreement explicitly prohibited the granting of amnesty to members of the DRC M23 rebel group for international crimes, including sexual violence crimes.

- In Liberia, INL funded a GBV Justice Advisor, supported by the Ministry of Justice and embedded with its GBV prosecution unit. The Advisor provided expert advice on a range of strategic and technical matters related to GBV crimes, including prosecuting sexual assault, abuse, and exploitation cases. The GBV Justice Advisor also helped develop standards and procedures for operations, administrations, victim-witness coordination, and case management.

- In Rwanda, the African Bureau's Africa-Women, Peace and Security program is a local civil society organization that has trained over 1,000 men, women, boys, and girls at a department-funded community center in rural Rulindo district on anti-GBV tactics and public perceptions. Trainings focus on the behavioral change of men and boys, accountability, and public awareness.

South and Central Asia:

- Shelters funded by the Department of State in Afghanistan served over 2,000 women and children in 2013 by providing legal aid, education, health care and related services. A key challenge facing women's shelters in Afghanistan is the reintegration into society of shelter beneficiaries unable to return to their families. In 2013, the Department of State awarded a grant to fund three transitional houses to address this problem. The transitional houses will provide education and vocational training to survivors of gender-based violence, with the goal of supporting beneficiaries to work outside the shelter.

Western Hemisphere:

- Through a Memorandum of Understanding (MOU) between the New York City Police Department (NYPD), and INL, NYPD officers worked to build the capacity of the Child Protection Unit of the Haitian National Police (HNP) to address gender-based and domestic violence against children. The NYPD and HNP community-policing unit implemented after school programs for underprivileged children and is engaged in reaching out to at risk children in various neighborhoods of Port au Prince. For the first time under this MOU, there have been joint community outreach efforts between the HNP child protection unit and the Gender Based Violence unit. INL has also established MOUs with various other U.S. law enforcement agencies to conduct training on gender-based violence and sex crimes for police officers in Trinidad and Tobago, Dominica, Grenada, and at the International Law Enforcement Academy in Budapest, Hungary. Future training in the Eastern Caribbean is in the planning phase.

- In Costa Rica, INL supports improving access to forensic services for victims of sexual assault, and trains police and EMT responders in victims' services. INL supports another program in the North Atlantic Autonomous Region of Nicaragua that trains local

Nicaraguan NGOs on the particulars of a recently-passed anti-GBV law and how best to advocate for women within that new legal framework.

- Through the Merida Initiative in Mexico, INL is training first responders on properly addressing and documenting incidents of gender-based violence, providing support to Women's Centers and Shelters, and making resources available to survivors. In addition, in northern Mexico, DRL is supporting a program that provides legal and psychological services to survivors of gender-based violence. <u>Since September 2010, 1,015 women have received support from the program.</u> Some of the program participants have gone on to form self-help groups to support other women in similar circumstances.

East Asia and the Pacific:

- The United States Department of Justice (DOJ) International Criminal Investigative Training Assistance Program's (ICITAP's) Indonesia Women's Leadership Development Project (WLDP) provides a platform for the promotion of women's issues within the criminal justice sector in Indonesia. DOJ ICITAP WLDP has trained Indonesian National Police (INP) personnel and has conducted two @america events, one of which was *Suffering in Silence-Women as Victims of Domestic Violence and Sexual Abuse*, promoting the value of women within the Indonesian criminal justice system, and specifically addressing issues facing victims of crime and violence.

Advancing the Role of Women in Peace and Security:

Implementing the U.S. National Action Plan on Women, Peace, and Security. Developed in 2011, the National Action Plan lays out the United States' strategy for integrating women's views and perspectives fully into our diplomatic, security, and development efforts. The strategy envisions women not simply as beneficiaries, but as agents of peace, reconciliation, development, growth, and stability. In working to implement the strategy, the United States has engaged international partners and civil society organizations across the globe to empower women as equal partners in preventing conflict and building peace. Furthermore, through humanitarian diplomacy and assistance, the United States promotes women's equal access to relief and recovery resources, advocates for their participation in managing those resources, and works to better address the needs of women and girls. Efforts to implement the National Action Plan include the following:

- **Releasing a Guide to Gender in the Criminal Justice System.** Historically, women have been excluded from, and under-served in, criminal justice sector institutions, and they have often faced discrimination and violence based on their gender. As part of the U.S. government's commitment to reversing this trend, INL, in consultation with S/GWI, developed the *INL Guide to Gender in the Criminal Justice System*. The Guide provides technical guidance to INL staff designing and implementing programs that promote and incorporate gender mainstreaming in all areas of the criminal justice system. After taking stock of the political, cultural, and legal considerations in a given country, the Guide encourages INL assistance implementers to rethink long-established practices and require them to evaluate the positive and negative consequences a proposed intervention will have on women and men.

- **Requiring Gender Analysis in Calls for Proposals.** In support of the U.S. National Action Plan on Women Peace and Security, which calls for gender integration to promote gender equality and improve programming and policy outcomes, beginning in FY 2014, PRM is requiring its non-governmental organization (NGO) partners to include a gender analysis in all project proposals in order to better meet the unique needs of women and girls and identify and mitigate risks posed by gender dynamics. In addition, since 2000, PRM has provided more than $86 million in targeted assistance to help prevent and respond to GBV. The Department has encouraged partners to integrate efforts to address gender-based violence in both multi-sector and GBV-specific programming.

- **Increasing the Gender Network and Sharing Best Practices on Gender and Conflict.** In order to advance the status of women and girls and respond to gender-sensitive conflicts, the Bureau of Conflict and Stabilization Operations (CSO) partners with bilateral, host nations, civil society, practitioners, academia, and the private sector to promote gender equality. Through gender-related events, CSO has developed a network of core gender experts who can be called upon for technical assistance and guidance. Furthermore, the Department's relationship with Justice Rapid Response (JRR) has given the United States access to a number of GBV experts who can rapidly deploy to conflict zones when needed.

Expanding Women's Political Participation and Empowering Women as Partners in Preventing Conflict and Building Peace:

- The Department of State and USAID helped build the political participation capacity of approximately 700 Syrian women through training in negotiation, leadership, advocacy, and other skills. The U.S. government also facilitated the creation of the Syrian Women's Network, which was one of several Syrian women's civil society groups that became an instrumental advocate for women and civil society in the Geneva 2 peace negotiations. The United States has also promoted Syrian women's inclusion in Syrian peace negotiations through ongoing diplomatic efforts.

- The U.S. government frequently worked with and called on the Yemeni government to adhere to commitments to ensure women's participation in Yemen's National Dialogue and political transition. Subsequently, women represented approximately 30 percent of the 565 delegates participating in Yemen's National Dialogue process. The dialogue brought together Yemenis from across the political spectrum for the most inclusive discussion of its kind in Yemen's history. Women also joined nine working groups within the Dialogue to discuss governance, state-building, deep-seated regional grievances, human rights, and security. The Department of State also supported the participation of young women in the National Youth Shadow Dialogue to ensure the integration of Yemeni youth's policy priorities into the National Dialogue process.

- Through conflict analysis, CSO discovered that, in order to increase women's participation, efforts warranted diplomatic and grassroots initiatives. CSO field officers helped to shape Embassy Rangoon's "Strategic Paper on Gender and Women's Empowerment." This framework provides guidance on gender equity and increased participation of women in public life, including in the peace process and inter-communal peace initiatives in Burma. In the summer of 2013, CSO helped to empower Burmese women in civil society organizations to support peace initiatives by organizing and conducting a series of women's roundtables throughout the country to gauge women's views and concerns about their role in public life.

Expanding Training for Women in Criminal Justice Fields. INL programs support efforts to advance gender equality and social inclusion within host nation law enforcement, correctional, and judicial institutions by helping countries hire, train, and retain more female law enforcement and justice sector officials, and promote fair and equal employment practices. For example, in Pakistan, INL has trained 57 female prosecutors, including 100 percent of women prosecutors in Khyber Pakhtunkhwa province and 75 percent of women prosecutors in Balochistan. In Haiti, INL is working with the HNP to recruit more female cadets. INL is also currently supporting a year-long training of ten female HNP cadets in Colombia; this training focuses on gender-based violence and child protection issues. In Tajikistan, INL is providing gender awareness training to law enforcement, government, and community representatives.

Training Women in Countering Terrorism. The Anti-Terrorism Assistance (ATA) program, a partnership between the State Department's Bureau of Counterterrorism and the Bureau of Diplomatic Security, is now tracking the number of women trained in each partner nation through the use of Nonproliferation, Anti-terrorism, Demining, and Related Activities (NADR)/ATA funding. The ATA program also trains units of female law enforcement officers in several countries, and attempts to recruit American women instructors to teach ATA curriculum. Finally, ATA is making changes to ATA curriculum to emphasize the particular need to protect women in the course of counterterrorism investigations and operations.

Supporting Drug Addiction Treatment Programs for Women. Rampant drug use is a public security issue. In post-conflict societies, drug treatment and prevention is part of the reconstruction process and works as a strategy to prevent the deterioration of governance and economic development. The State Department has undertaken efforts to support addiction prevention and treatment programs for women in Afghanistan, Liberia, Mexico, South Africa, and other Latin America countries and plans to launch additional efforts throughout Africa and Asia in 2014. Efforts include training both regional and national trainers to disseminate and implement INL's Guiding the Recovery of Women (GROW) curriculum, distributing information to the public, translating the curriculum into other languages to reach other countries, developing training, and coordinating the response of public institutions along with NGOs.

Empowering Women and Girls:

Advancing the Equal Futures Partnership. The Department of State assisted in expanding membership from 12 to 24 member partner countries, working with them to develop concrete actions that would advance women's economic and political participation. The Equal Futures Partnership is a multilateral initiative designed to empower women economically and politically. Equal Futures partners commit to take actions including legal, regulatory, and policy reforms to ensure women fully participate in public life and that they lead and benefit from inclusive economic growth.

Empowering Women and Girls through Educational and Professional Exchange Programs. Exchange programs supported by the Department of State reach women and girls from across the globe, improving their professional and personal prospects through a variety of programs, such as those targeting women in technology from across the Middle East and North Africa, athletes and sports managers in Brazil, and women entrepreneurs from Africa and the Americas. In 2013, just over 50 percent of the Department's 360,000 exchange participants were women—many from societies where opportunities for women and girls are limited.

Women and the Economy. The State Department is continuing efforts to strengthen networks of women entrepreneurs such as the African Women's Entrepreneurship Program (AWEP), Women's Entrepreneurship in the Americas (WEAmericas), Invest for the Future, and the South and Central Asia Women's Entrepreneurship Networks. These efforts include hosting a delegation of AWEP women to the United States, funding training, and sponsoring an AWEP conference on the margins of the African Growth Opportunity Act (AGOA) ministerial in Addis Ababa, in August 2013. In September 2013, the Department advanced the agenda of Asia Pacific Economic Cooperation (APEC) Women and the Economy Forum, along with hosting fora on women and technology, women and government procurement, women's access to capital with finance ministers, and advising economies on developing their own strategic plans for integrating women in the economy. In May 2013, the Department hosted a second delegation of women entrepreneurs from Latin America through the WEAmericas initiative and in July 2013 co-funded a joint initiative with New Zealand focused on women in agriculture in the Pacific and Caribbean Islands to address shared challenges and best practices.

Leading Global Efforts to Advance Gender Equality and Strengthening Multilateral Organizations:

Promoting Women's Rights in the UN Commission on the Status of Women (CSW). At the March 2013 CSW session, member states adopted Agreed Conclusions on "The elimination and prevention of all forms of violence against women and girls." The document recognizes that respecting and protecting sexual and reproductive health and reproductive rights are essential to preventing, mitigating, and eliminating violence against women and girls. It calls for increased protection for groups facing increased risks of violence, including women and girls with disabilities; women and girls living with HIV/AIDS; and indigenous women and girls. It states that customs, traditions, and religious considerations cannot be used to justify harmful traditional practices such as female genital mutilation/cutting and forced and early marriage. The Agreed Conclusions also reaffirms the critical role of women human rights defenders.

Promoting Women's Rights in the UN Human Rights Council (HRC). The United States co-sponsored the June 2013 HRC resolution on "Accelerating Efforts to Eliminate All Forms of Violence Against Women: Preventing and Responding to Rape and Other Forms of Sexual Violence Against Women." The United States delivered a General Statement emphasizing the importance of comprehensive support services for survivors of violence; the need to prevent and respond to intimate partner violence; and the connection between sexual and reproductive health and reproductive rights and efforts to address violence against women. The United States co-sponsored the September 2013 HRC resolutions on "Strengthening Efforts to Prevent and Eliminate Child, Early and Forced Marriage: Challenges, Achievements, Best Practices and Implementation Gaps" – the UN's first stand-alone resolution on the topic – and "Special Rapporteur on Contemporary Forms of Slavery, Including its Causes and Consequences." The Special Rapporteur works on such critical issues as sexual slavery, child slavery, forced and early marriage, and debt bondage, and the latter resolution renewed the Special Rapporteur's mandate for the next three years. The U.S. government also co-sponsored a September 2013 HRC decision to hold a panel discussion on female genital mutilation/cutting.

Promoting Women's Rights in the UN General Assembly (UNGA). During the fall 2013 UNGA, the United States co-sponsored the resolutions on "Child, Early, and Forced Marriage;" "The Girl Child;" "Improvement of the Situation of Women in Rural Areas;" "Violence Against Women Migrant Workers;" and "Women Human Rights Defenders." The United States also joined consensus on the Chair's Text on "Follow-Up to the Fourth World Conference on Women and full implementation of the Beijing Declaration and Platform for Action and the Outcome of the Twenty-Third Special Session of the General Assembly."

Supporting UN Women. The United States holds a seat on the Executive Board of the UN Entity for Gender Equality and Women's Empowerment (UN Women). For FY 2013, the United States contributed $7.2 million to UN Women's core budget. U.S. funding also supports UN Women programs in Mozambique and Tanzania to address violence against women and girls. In addition, U.S. monies support UN Women's role in the UN Safe Cities Initiative, working with civil society organizations in New Delhi to make the city safer for women.

Promoting Women's Critical Role in Clean Energy Solutions to Climate Change. The Department of State launched the Partnership on Women's Entrepreneurship in Renewables ("wPOWER") in January 2013. wPOWER aims to empower more than 8,000 women clean energy entrepreneurs across East Africa, Nigeria, and India who will deliver clean energy access to more than 3.5 million people over the next three years. To reach this goal, the Department of State and USAID have teamed up with the MacArthur Foundation, the Global Alliance for Clean Cookstoves, CARE International, Solar Sister, Swayam Shikshan Prayog, the Wangari Maathai Institute for Peace & Environmental Studies (WMI), Women for Women International, and the

Green Belt Movement to provide training, access to clean energy technology inventories, and micro-finance loans to wPOWER participants.

Empowering Women and Girls in Specific Regions. The Department of State works in all regions of the world to advance the status of women and girls through policy and programming. Specific program examples include:

South and Central Asia:

- The Department of State implemented a program in Afghanistan, Pakistan, and Bangladesh promoting women's rights by <u>providing 450 imams</u> with an educational curriculum on women's rights. As a result of this program, awareness about women's rights appears to have improved, and imams have been speaking out about women's rights in Islam and women's inheritance rights, and have been condemning violence against women.

- In 2013, the Department of State launched a regional women's entrepreneurship initiative in South Asia as follow-on to the 2012 South Asia Women's Entrepreneurship Symposium. This initiative aims to increase access to finance, markets, information, and training for businesswomen by building regional connectivity. The initiative has already advanced policy change in Sri Lanka by helping to implement a new policy of providing collateral-free loans to women entrepreneurs. A similar regional initiative was launched in Central Asia (Afghanistan) in 2012.

- The U.S. Embassy in Dushanbe has undertaken an initiative to address food security in Tajikistan by concentrating on female-headed households. This initiative seeks to increase the participation of women in commercial farming, and Embassy Dushanbe has supported a community development project that aims to involve both women and youth in more active roles in resolving community problems. The Embassy is also relying on local women leaders to help improve women's land rights, giving more female farmers the opportunity to farm land, and encouraging women to seek leadership positions in their own communities. Another successful project in this initiative <u>worked with local woman leaders to provide nutrition education training to 1,000 women in 50 villages throughout Tajikistan in the last two years alone.</u>

Western Hemisphere

- Through two interagency agreements, the Bureau of Western Hemisphere Affairs and the Inter-American Foundation support historically marginalized groups in the Western Hemisphere through technical assistance, training, and education, as part of the Americas Partnership for Social Inclusion and Equality (APSIE) and the Inter-American Social Protection Network (IASPN). Under these agreements, the Department of State is currently funding projects in Brazil, Colombia, Ecuador, Guatemala, and Peru. These projects, which are focused on women's empowerment, support leadership and are often coupled with economic development among indigenous, African descendent, and rural women.

- In Honduras, as part of efforts to counter a gang-driven homicide crisis, CSO is supporting local activists to form "Mujeres Unidas," a group of women who have lost a loved one to violence. The goal of this group is to help women recognize they have a voice, their loved ones are not forgotten, and the government needs to bring justice to each case. At the event announcing the launch of "Mujeres Unidas," more than 100 women brought photos of their loved ones and banners demanding government action. The international and local media came out in force, including media outlets from Mexico and Costa Rica.

Near East:

- In Iraq, the Bureau of Democracy, Human Rights and Labor funded a program that launched the first ever female-owned commercial advertising agency. The agency works to advance women's role in the media industry and cultivates cutting edge reporting on women's political, economic, and social participation.

East Asia and the Pacific:

- The U.S. Embassy Small Grants Program received $1 million via the Abbott Fund's partnership with the Secretary of State's International Fund for Women and Girls to empower women and girls in Burma. To date, Embassy Rangoon has funded nine projects that focus on underprivileged or conflict-affected areas and promote women and peace-building, women's leadership, women and girls' empowerment, women's health, and addressing gender-based violence.

White House Council on Women and Girls
Recent Accomplishments of the Department of Treasury
March 2014

Establishing Community Development Financial Institutions (CDFI) Focused on Women-Owned Small Businesses and Women Entrepreneurs. The Treasury Department funds several CDFI's that are exclusively focused on lending to woman-owned small businesses and women entrepreneurs. Two examples include the Wisconsin Woman's Business Initiative Corporation (http://www.wwbic.com/about-vision) and Women Venture (http://www.womenventure.org/about.html).

Making Loans to Low-Income Women Borrowers in Underserved Communities. The New Market Tax Credit (NMTC) Program supports investments that target low-income women in distressed communities. In FY 2012, NMTC allocatees made a total of $408 million in investments in women-owned or controlled businesses and $12 million worth of loans to low-income women borrowers. In addition, the CDFI Program has made 3,527 loans totaling $116 million to low-income women.

Expanding Opportunities to Provide Access to Capital for Women. Created by the Small Business Jobs Act of 2010, the Small Business Lending Fund (SBLF) is a dedicated fund designed to provide capital to qualified community banks and community development loan funds (CDLFs) to encourage small business lending. For the year ended June 30, 2012, 91 percent of SBLF participants reported outreach or advertising activities targeting women, veterans, or minority communities. In total, 76 percent of SBLF participants reported that they are members or participate in community organizations and/or trade associations that target women, veterans, or minority communities; 53 percent reported using paid advertisement or notices in print, radio, or electronic media to target women, veterans, or minority communities; and, 46 percent indicated that they distributed marketing materials targeting women, veterans, or minority communities. In total, participants reported expenditures of $16 million associated with small business-related outreach activities. Of this amount, $2.9 million was spent on outreach to women-owned businesses.

Supporting Women-Owned Businesses Through State-Based Efforts. The State Small Business Credit Initiative (SSBCI) was funded with $1.5 billion from the Small Business Jobs

Act of 2010 to strengthen state programs that make loans to small businesses and small manufacturers. Under SSBCI, states designed their own credit support programs. Some of these programs directly target women-owned businesses; others are not targeted at women but have resulted in expanded access to credit for women-owned small businesses.

Supporting Women-Owned Business Through Treasury Contracting. The Office of Minority and Women Inclusion employs a number of strategies to engage women-owned businesses about contracting opportunities at Treasury. In FY 2013, Treasury awarded $257 million in contracts to women-owned businesses regardless of size. Additionally, based on FY 2013 preliminary data, Treasury attained more than double its Small Business Administration-set women-owned small business goal of 5 percent for three consecutive years.

White House Council on Women and Girls
Recent Accomplishments of U.S. Agency for International Development
March 2014

Preventing and Responding to Gender-Based Violence (GBV) in the Democratic Republic of Congo. USAID's GBV care and treatment programs in the Democratic Republic of Congo increase access to medical, psychological, social, legal, and economic support services for survivors. These programs also seek to improve community awareness of the types and consequences of GBV. In FY 2013, USAID's social protection programs alone reached 9,264 GBV survivors with social services, trained 4,258 service providers working with GBV survivors, and strengthened 926 local organizations that serve GBV-affected populations.

Empowering Yemen Female Leaders During Historic Political Transition. USAID is helping Yemen pursue its transition to democracy by supporting the historic National Dialogue Conference. USAID provided targeted orientation training and mentoring for 129 female delegates to the National Dialogue Conference, including sessions on communications and advocacy, technical information about the Dialogue process, strategic planning, and a meeting with the Dialogue Technical Committee. The female delegates played a leading role throughout the Dialogue and were able to successfully negotiate a 30% quota for women across branches of government.

Changing the Way Women Access Justice in Guatemala Through new 24 Hour Court. In Guatemala, USAID is providing technical assistance, training, and equipment to operationalize a new specialized 24-hour court for cases related to violence against women, exploitation, sexual violence and human trafficking. The new model, one of the first in Latin America, includes a criminal court, a public defense office, a police substation, and a forensic clinic, and is staffed by prosecutors, psychologists, doctors, and lawyers. This integrated approach ensures victims receive the timely assistance they need and strengthens criminal investigation by using scientific evidence. Since the 24-hour court opened its doors, 846 protection measures for women and 307 arrest warrants have been authorized. In total, 125 people have been sent to prison for violence against women and sexual exploitation.

Strengthening USAID Staff Capacity in Gender Awareness and Sensitization. To date, more than 1,000 employees have been trained through a new on-line Gender 101 course or in-person regional trainings on the importance of addressing gender equality in programming to enhance development outcomes. In addition, through a mandatory orientation for new Civil Service and Foreign Service employees, more than 500 USAID personnel have been trained on the Counter-Trafficking in Persons policy and the Code of Conduct.

Developing Innovative Public Private Partnerships using Media and Engagement for Social Change. USAID has developed three new innovative Public Private Partnerships using multi-media tools such as documentary film, mobile games and short videos along with local grassroots engagement campaigns to promote global gender equality. These three campaigns – Half the Sky, Women and Girls Lead Global, and Girl Rising – aim to spur public dialogue; create positive shifts in attitudes and behavior; and nurture institutional policy changes to support gender equality. Altogether, the campaigns will be implemented in 11 different countries—India, Bangladesh, Jordan, Egypt, Kenya, Nigeria, Congo, Malawi, Colombia, Peru, and El Salvador with the support of 16 resource partners including Goldman Sachs, Intel, Johnson and Johnson, CNN, Ford Foundation, Pearson Foundation, UN Foundation, The Documentary Group, Independent Television Service, and others.

Creating New Opportunities for Women and Girls in Afghanistan. USAID is launching a new five-year initiative, Promoting Gender Equity in National Priority Programs (2014-2019) to target the education, training and empowerment of a new generation of Afghan women, aged 18-30. The program will increase women's contributions to Afghanistan's development by bringing more women into decision-making positions in Afghanistan's public, private and civil society sectors. The program will achieve this objective by strengthening women's rights groups, boosting women's participation in the economy, helping women gain business, management and leadership skills, and more. The program is designed to empower a critical mass of Afghan women by solidifying the gains achieved over the past decade as the country enters a critical period of transition. It builds upon earlier USAID investments in education, health, democratic governance, civil society strengthening and economic growth. Through those investments, and of others, Afghanistan has seen one of the most rapid declines in maternal mortality anywhere in the world and an increase in life expectancy of 15-20 years. Girls now account for more than a third of all school children, compared to virtually none in 2002. More than 120,000 young women have finished secondary school, and 40,000 are working on university degrees. Women have also entered the business and political arenas with women now making up more than 25 percent of the Afghan parliament.

Making Pregnancy and Childbirth Safer in Uganda and Zambia. The USAID-led "Saving Mothers, Giving Life " (SMGL) public-private partnership has reduced the maternal mortality rate in target districts in Uganda by 30% and SMGL facilities in Zambia by 35% by strengthening country district health systems through health worker training, infrastructure improvements, and linkages to transportation. Through these interventions, the partnership has increased the number of births taking place in a health facility (by 62 percent in Uganda, and 35 percent in Zambia); increased the number of facilities offering basic emergency obstetric and newborn services; (by 200 percent in Uganda, and 100 percent in Zambia), and expanded testing and treatment for HIV/AIDS for the prevention of mother-to-child transmission of HIV (by 28 percent Uganda, and18 percent Zambia).

White House Council on Women and Girls
Recent Accomplishments of the U.S. Department of Agriculture
March 2014

Providing Nutrition Assistance and Breastfeeding Support. USDA's Supplemental Nutrition Program for Women, Infants and Children (WIC) program provided nutrition assistance and breastfeeding support to more than two million low-income pregnant, breastfeeding and postpartum women, as well as to their children. For the first time, the proportion of breastfeeding women exceeded that of non-breastfeeding postpartum women in the WIC program. In addition, USDA's Supplemental Nutrition Assistance Program (SNAP) lifted nearly 1.4 million households headed by single women out of poverty, including approximately 600,000 households headed by women with children.

Supporting Women-Owned Small Businesses and Entrepreneurs. In FY13, USDA awarded $381 million in contracts to Women Owned Small Businesses. In addition, USDA Marketing and Regulatory Programs (MRP) awarded approximately $30 million in commodity procurement contracts to women-owned small businesses. USDA's Rural Development office also provided grants to support female agricultural producers and entrepreneurs across the country.

Providing Nutrition Advice and Resources. USDA's website, ChooseMyPlate.gov, includes numerous topics for women. More than 70% of the audience using the website, online tools and MyPlate social media platforms are women, and many of the resources are designed for mothers with young children.

Conducted Educational Programs for Young Women and Girls. USDA has offered a variety of educational programs aimed at young women and girls including workshops on careers in science; a camp focused on natural resources career paths; an Environmental Leadership Institute; and roundtables to encourage girls to pursue science and agricultural careers.

Awarded Funding to Projects Supporting Female Farmers. USDA has supported a number of initiatives designed to help female farmers including education programs that focus on risk and financial management, crop insurance, marketing and estate planning. Examples include: A $98,959 grant to empower farm women in Iowa to be better farm business partners through networks and by managing and organizing critical information; and a $46,204.00 grant to ensure that 541 women producers in Missouri and Nebraska will increase their knowledge and understanding to make better decisions about crop insurance, marketing, financial management, estate planning and other risk management tools.

Conducting Nutrition and Education Programs for Girls Around the World:

Burkina Faso: Under the auspices of USDA's McGovern-Dole International Food for Education Program, Catholic Relief Services (CRS) has provided a daily hot meal to approximately 152,000 students in Burkina Faso, utilizing U.S.-grown commodities. USDA support has also allowed CRS to implement a community-driven mentoring activity that seeks to promote girls' education and prevent girls from dropping out of school. To date, 750 Burkinabe women have been trained on mentoring, girls' education, and gender, and 5,563 girls have been supported full-time by their mentors.

Pakistan: Land O'Lakes implemented a McGovern Dole school feeding program in Pakistan focused on improving elementary school enrollment and attendance among girls. Land O'Lakes provided a monthly take-home food ration to motivate regular attendance; helped re-open all girls elementary schools; and improved the health status of pregnant women, lactating mothers, and children by offering a monthly take-home ration as an incentive to utilize preventive services at community health centers. They also coordinated de-worming and annual medical and eyesight examinations; provided clean drinking water at schools; and taught good nutrition, hygiene, and health practices to students.

Nepal: With support from the McGovern-Dole Program, the World Food Programme (WFP) has been helping the Government of Nepal implement its school feeding program for children. WFP has provided monthly take-home rations of cooking oil to families who send their girl children to school, helping to offset the 'loss of hands' at home so girls can attend school instead of performing chores in the household. De-worming tablets are also provided to children in the school feeding program to help their bodies better absorb the micronutrients in the food. In Nepal's schools with WFP school feeding programs, girls' attendance rates have, on average, risen by 27 percent, and girls' enrollment has increased by 52 percent. Both children and teachers report improvements in cognitive and learning abilities.

Afghanistan: USDA has partnered with World Vision to deliver a McGovern-Dole girls' education project in the mountainous, western provinces of Ghor, Herat and Badghis. In 2003, before this program began, the Afghanistan Ministry of Education reported that fewer than 9,000 girls and only 27,000 boys attended schools in these provinces. With consistent support from USDA's McGovern-Dole Program, school attendance has grown in 266 schools across the provinces. Girls' attendance in particular has increased by tens of thousands of girls, representing a 98 percent increase. A key aspect of USDA's girl-centric project implementation is take-home food rations which are contingent on girls' attendance records. In addition, to help address family resource constraints, USDA provides school classroom kit packages for girls, including writing supplies and basic learning tools.

White House Council on Women and Girls
Recent Accomplishments of the U.S. Trade Representative
March 2014

Mainstreaming Women in the Economy Policy Issues. USTR, working closely with USAID and State used bilateral and regional meetings of our Trade and Investment Framework Agreements (TIFA) to encourage a dialogue on what US and TIFA partners are doing to encourage/support women and women owned businesses to participate in the global economy. Our works mainstreams policy discussions to support women owned businesses to participate in trade, particularly in sub-Sahara Africa and South Asia.

Forging a Memorandum of Understanding (MOU) with Afghanistan. This MOU sets out how the U.S. and Afghanistan will work together to encourage greater involvement of women in trade and investment. MOUs on women's empowerment with other regional trading partners are being considered, and women's issues are an agenda item in all TIFA meetings throughout the South and Central Asia region.

Encouraging Women's Entrepreneurship Around the World. USTR supported the Administration's efforts to increase the participation of women under our trade preference program, Africa Growth and Opportunity Act (AGOA), via the African Women's Entrepreneurship Program (AWEP). USTR staff used a series of trade- and investment-related meetings as opportunities to hold workshops and consultations with AWEP participants from throughout sub-Saharan Africa. USTR also used its Trade and Investment Council meetings, and meetings related to free trade agreements, to promote more openness in Middle East and North Africa MENA trade and investment policies which helps help create opportunities for women in MENA countries. For example, in the Tunisia Small and Medium Enterprise program launched by USTR and USAID under the MENA US-Tunisia Bilateral Action Plan, the Women's Heads of Business National Chamber (Chambre Nationale des Femmes Chefs d'Entreprises (CNFCE) have been trained in the U.S. model of Small Business Development Centers (SBDCs) and selected for a Tunisia SBDC pilot. In addition, USTR continues to work with the State Department on Burma/Myanmar, and more broadly in the region, to advance rule of law and create opportunities in regional and global markets for women entrepreneurs and business owners.

White House Council on Women and Girls
Recent Accomplishments of the Department of Veteran Affairs
March 2014

Launched a New Department-wide Women Veterans Program. In September 2012, VA launched a new Department-wide Women Veterans Program (WVP) to better coordinate and enhance access to, and delivery of, VA benefits and services for women Veterans. In the first year, this new WVP structure has improved collaboration and consistency in Department-wide operational activity, as well as engagement with, and communication to, women Veterans. Further, through the WVP, VA deployed innovative and evidence-based employee training that has improved understanding of women's military contributions and raised awareness of the importance of cultural competency in providing quality service to Veterans.

Delivered Unprecedented Levels of Benefits for Women Veterans. In fiscal year (FY) 2013, VA delivered benefits to significantly more women Veterans, including: compensation benefits to 329,390 women Veterans (up 9 percent); education benefits to 122,000 women Veterans (up 14 percent); and pension benefits to 12,651 women Veterans (held steady with FY 2012). VA also provided $1.9 billion in home loan guaranty benefits to 32,921 women Veterans (up 28 percent) and admitted 17,741 women Veterans to the vocational rehabilitation and employment program (up 8 percent). As of November 2013, the Veterans Retraining Assistance Program has successfully aided over 12,542 unemployed women Veterans with up to 12 months of training assistance. In addition, in FY 2013, VA's grant rates on disability claims for Posttraumatic Stress Disorder (PTSD) based on Military Sexual Trauma (MST) achieved parity with grant rates for all other PTSD claims. This was accomplished through an extensive claims staff training program, updated policies, and the efforts of specially-trained coordinators deployed throughout the country. Prior to this initiative, the grant rate for PTSD claims based on MST was substantially lower than all other PTSD claims, and variances in the accuracy were identified.

Delivered Quality Health Care to an Unprecedented Number of Women Veterans. In FY 2013, VA delivered high-quality health care to 390,000 women Veterans, a 10 percent increase over FY 2012. Recent, VA quality and safety data revealed that the quality of care provided to women Veterans through VA has been significantly higher than in the private sector, based on both gender-specific measures (e.g., screening for cervical and breast cancer) and for gender-neutral measures (e.g., management of hypertension and diabetes, treatment of elevated cholesterol, and screening for colorectal cancer).

Launched a Women Veterans Hotline. In FY 2013, VA expanded its outreach to women Veterans through a new hotline (1-855-VA-WOMEN) to respond to questions from Veterans, their families and caregivers about the many VA services and resources available to women Veterans. This hotline enhanced an outbound-only call center, improving responsiveness to women Veterans' needs. The service began accepting calls in April 2013 and, as of the end of FY 2013, more 20,000 women veterans' calls were received.

Expanded Research on Women Veterans' Health. In FY 2013, VA Research invested more than $16.5 million in 86 studies on women veterans' health. This research investment greatly expands VA's network of sites conducting women veterans' health research from four in 2010 to 37 in 2013, and the research being conducted may involve as many as 100,000 women Veterans. VA also funded Women's Health Collaborative Research to Enhance and Advance Transformation and Excellence (CREATE), a research initiative aimed at better meeting the needs of women Veterans.

www.ingramcontent.com/pod-product-compliance
Lightning Source LLC
Chambersburg PA
CBHW080851010626
R18375900001B/R183759PG45790CBX00009B/17